Tied to the Soul

*To Stella
Enjoy
Eva G Headley
xxx*

A Novel By

Eva G. Headley

The Write to Inspire Publishing
www.thewritetoinspire.com

ISBN: 978-0-9569742-0-4

Cover design by Jonathan Johnson of Brand Concept Creative Media
Edited by Shonell Bacon

First edition 2011
Printed in the United Kingdom

Published by:
The Write to Inspire Publishing Co.
CAN Mezzanine
49 - 51 East Road
London
N1 6AH

Praise for Tied to the Soul...

"We all have experienced doing something that didn't sit right with our souls and dealing with the consequences of those actions. This experience is what will connect readers to Headley's *Tied to the Soul*. It is a work that illustrates not only how we come to make the decisions (sometimes bad decisions) we do, but also how we can spend a lifetime suffering from those decisions For a realistic look at how we try to deal with the ups and downs of life and love, you should definitely check out Eva G. Headley's *Tied to the Soul*."

~ Shonell Bacon, author of Death at the Double Inkwell, founding editor of CLG Entertainment

Eva G. Headley's *Tied to the Soul* reminds us that love is often complicated but worth it. Through engaging and imperfect characters, she weaves a divinely orchestrated, unpredictable journey of regrets, redemption and restoration. Ms. Headley shines with her debut novel, establishing her place as a new and rising literary star. A must read for those who love contemporary inspirational fiction.

~ Norma L. Jarrett *Essence* Bestselling Author of *Sunday Brunch, Sunday Brunch Diaries* and *Sweet Magnolia*

Dedication

Tied to the Soul is dedicated to four of the most inspiring and beautiful women in my life: Elaine Robinson – Grandmother, Angela Robinson – Mother, Kate Ntem – Sister-Mother-Friend, and Fabie Gumbs – My Little Sister.

Acknowledgements

I would firstly like to thank God for inspiring me to write the way I do and pushing me to continue even when I doubted the gift placed in me. I will forever be your handmaiden.

Mentors are very important and precious and I would like to thank Michelle McKinney Hammond for always being there. This novel was planted in me at the DIVA conference in Chicago 2007. It took a minute to birth out, but I thank you for being someone I can look up to and aspire to.

Irene Myrtle Forrester (Cissy), thank you for believing in my dream. Even in the midst of adversity, you have been there through the whole process. Through my tears you have prayed for me, through my fears you have encouraged me, through my joys you have laughed with me. You are a true friend and most of all a true sister.

I would like to acknowledge a very special person who read the first ten pages of my novel before it was even finished, Essence bestselling Author Norma L Jarrett. Thank you for taking the time out to encourage me and let me know I had a gift. The prayers and encouragement have reminded me that God was in control.

A big thank-you goes to my fantastic editor, Shonell Bacon for doing more than what was required of her; there is no better editor in the world. You understand me as a writer and that is so important. Thank you, Keshia Dawn, for the divine hook-up. You have been such a blessing in my life.

In addition, I would like to thank the many pastors who have prayed with me through this process. Only God knows how thankful I am to you all. To all my friends and family who encouraged me on the way, you know who you are – Thank you.

There are many musical artists who inspired many scenes in this novel. So a big thank-you to Kirk Whalum, Will Downing, Gerald Albright, CeCe Winans, Chante Moore, Marvin Sapp, Mary Mary, Isley Brothers, Anita Baker, Boyz II Men, Hi-Five and the late Wayman Tisdale for making great, beautiful and inspiring music.

Chapter One

*R*ia had been leaning out of her bedroom window for the past half hour, observing the many people that walked along her street, some laughing, some enjoying the gentle Californian breeze as they walked casually. But they all seemed to be heading to a destination. She closed her eyes and felt the gentle sea breeze caress her face. It felt good to her and seemed to calm the storm that was brewing inside of her. She remembered the fearless determination she had back in her youth to get out and pursue her dreams of becoming a magazine editor. Now, staring at her dream, Ria felt like she was in a rut and she needed to get out of the season she was in.

She had moved into Shawn's house seven years ago, living like husband and wife, without any sign of a proposal. Lately, it seemed that they argued almost every day; this was not what she had bargained for. Her curvy size 12 had shrunken to a size 10 due to the emotional strain the arguing was having on her. Things weren't like they used to be. The flowers stopped coming, the spontaneous picnics and lovemaking became nonexistent. Shawn had changed and it seemed they were just living as roommates.

Ria walked from the window to the closet in order to change out of Shawn's old T-shirt. It was a Saturday afternoon and she had completed her housecleaning for the day. As she opened the closet door, she reviewed the reflection of her face in the door's cracked mirror. She ran her fingers past her smooth brown oval face and across her slanted eyes.

Should I put on a little make-up? Ria asked herself. She knew Shawn was coming home soon, and even though they were going through a rough patch, she still knew how to impress him. *Where's that lip gloss?*

Ria opened a small drawer and rumbled through the other make-up items before she pulled out her lip gloss. She dabbed the cushion tip of the pearly white sticky liquid on her lip and puckered her full lips together. She pulled out her hair pin and stretched over to place it on the dressing table next to the closet. She combed her shoulder-length hair down in an effort to make herself look other than a housewife. She changed herself into a white fitted top and a pair of stone washed jeans. She looked back on her dresser and saw a white letter folded up. She was once again reminded of a choice she had to make. Ria had left the letter on the dresser and tried to distract herself by cleaning the apartment top to bottom. She picked up the paper again and read it. *We would like to offer you the editor's position at Exhale Magazine...* Her eyes jumped to another part of the letter: *...relocation to New York.*

Her slanted dark brown eyes repeatedly jumped from the two sentences. Ria held the letter in her hand, the opportunity of taking her career to the next level balanced with leaving the love her life behind was becoming a difficult decision to weigh up. *Exhale* was a successful publication that uniquely appealed to a diverse female audience. A smaller office was located in Los Angeles where Ria was based, but the headquarters was in New York. She loved working there as the editor's assistant. She gave it her all. It was merely a blessing doing the job she was doing. Ever since she was a little girl, she had a brilliant sense of creativity and a keen eye for detail.

After Ria had finished college, she worked for the men's suit department in Macy's for a year and half. She happened to assist a gentleman named James Daniels who was the CEO of Exhale magazine; she told him of her dreams of being in the publishing industry. He in turn offered her an interview to be his assistant, which she got on the same day. It had been eight years since then and she had worked her butt off to get the editor's assistant position. But she knew that she could do more.

Looking around her bedroom, her eyes glazed over everything she was so very familiar with—the squeaky bed, the broken down closet. She knew what her heart told her to do, and she already knew what she had to sacrifice.

At twenty-nine, Ria realized that she wasn't getting any younger, and she was tired of barely making it from paycheck to paycheck. Los Angeles was not a cheap place to reside. And more so, she was tired of living off of Shawn. She wanted something of her own, something *she* had worked for. She knew this letter would open doors that she had only dreamt of, and she could not let this opportunity pass her by.

At the sound of Shawn's car pulling into the driveway, Ria snapped out of her thoughts. She hesitated as though she had the whole world tied to her neck. She folded up the letter and tucked it in her notebook as if to tuck the issue out of sight.

"Ria!" Shawn shouted.

As she came down the stairs, she looked at Shawn, and for some reason he looked more handsome than he did that morning. She stopped a few steps from the bottom before she continued to descend down the stairs. Ria observed how he kept his hair trim, just the way she liked it. She observed his 6'4 muscular caramel frame and his broad back as he bent down to loosen his sneakers. As she stretched her arms and rose on her toes to compensate for her 5'9" height to embrace his broad shoulders, she lightly traced her hands over the back of his head. Shawn returned her embrace with a gentle kiss on the forehead. Ria could tell from his loose embrace that he was tired from working out at the gym, and did not want any arguments. The petty argument they had shared earlier that morning still slightly annoyed her. Ria decided to push it out of her mind and be optimistic.

"Guess what, baby?" Ria asked. She hated keeping secrets from Shawn.

"What?"

"I got a reply back from the magazine opening I applied for."

"The one in New York?" Shawn said.

"Yeah that one. They offered me the editor's position." Ria felt

Shawn's eyes pierced into her like a laser.

"That's great," he said bluntly while loosening Ria's hold around his neck. He marched toward the kitchen and opened the refrigerator, taking the carton of orange juice into his muscular hands. He carelessly drank from it and dumped it back into the refrigerator, allowing drips of orange juice to fall into the compartment.

Ria ground her teeth together in order to stop her from going on a nagging rant. She had spent hours cleaning the refrigerator. She ignored Shawn's attempt to annoy her; she was determined not to have an argument.

"Is that all you have to say? That's great? It's a great opportunity for me, baby. I have only dreamed of an opportunity like this."

"So you gonna move to New York, huh? Who do you know in New York?" Shawn asked Ria as he folded his arms in front of him.

Ria walked over to Shawn and took hold of one of his hands and cradled it in hers.

"Look, this will only be for a little while, Shawn. We need the money and I cannot just keep on depending on you for everything. I want bigger and better things in life than this."

Ria knew that her move could be more permanent than just a little while. But she knew if she communicated this, the argument about her future could take a turn for the worst.

"What are you trying to say, Ria? Oh, I see how it goes. You got your high paying opportunity, and you want to ditch me for your better life—is that what all the arguments have been about for the past two months? You wanting to get out?"

"I can't believe you. I thought you of all people would want the best for me." Ria said.

"It's all about you. It's all about Ria having to get this, and Ria trying to get that. What about us, huh?" Shawn said.

Ria gave Shawn a look that was so sharp and cold, it could freeze hell. "You cannot be serious." Ria laughed sarcastically. "It's all about me, huh? So who is it about when I'm cleaning your clothes, cooking your food, making sure this home stays in order?"

Shawn and Ria stood face to face as though they were posing for a boxing match.

"No Shawn, let me tell you how it is—" Ria stopped in mid-sentence. She took a deep breath to calm herself down. To stop herself from slapping Shawn across his face, she pressed her frustrated fingers against her forehead and shifted her attention to a small stain on the kitchen linoleum. The tension in the atmosphere weighed a ton, and the extra weight threatened Ria with an impending migraine.

"I really need you to support me on this, Shawn. Maybe the break will be good for us," she said flatly. "You know I love you and no amount of distance is going to tear us apart." Ria said.

"Well, it's your life. Do what you want with it." Shawn strode off from where Ria was standing and went to sit on the couch to watch TV. Ria stood there with her hand on her hip. She knew that if this argument continued, she might end up leaving that night for good.

As Ria turned to the warm cooking pots that housed the food she had prepared earlier, she contemplated whether to serve Shawn his food. She knew if she didn't, it would be like adding wood to the fire. "Well I'm definitely sick of this crap," Ria muttered to herself and placed the plate into the microwave.

*****

The living room to which Shawn entered in reflected his mood. The curtains were drawn, not allowing the remaining evening sun to peek through. He grabbed the remote control from the couch and sat down placing one foot on the coffee table. Another habit Ria could not stand and he knew it. Shawn sat flicking through the channels, his mind busy on the news Ria had told him. He glanced at her as she dished out his food and placed it in the microwave. Despite their current disagreements, Ria was still the love of his life. He knew from the moment he met her in college that she was the one who would capture his heart. What he loved about her was

that she was a fighter, and she knew how to get what she wanted. How ironic that the very thing he loved about her seemed to be tearing them apart.

Life was fast in New York, and he pondered about other men approaching Ria—with her cat-shaped eyes, voluptuous figure, and teasing smile, he was sure that she'd spark a few interests. Would she leave him for a man that could give her what he couldn't? His thoughts began to unsettle him. He knew that their relationship had been going through a turbulent period. Maybe this was a sign that the foundations they both were trying to hold together were breaking.

"Thanks," Shawn said as Ria presented him with a smoking plate of food.

"I'm going to Chanel's," Ria said as she left the room.

"What time are you coming back?"

"The time I get in." Ria said sharply.

Before Shawn could reply, he heard the front door slam.

Chapter Two

R ia stopped outside her front door after slamming it shut. She took her time to cool herself down. She did not want to end up driving like a mad woman and be stopped by the cops. She took two deep breaths while counting to ten.

Once Ria reached her car, she opened it and took one glance up at her apartment window. She cut her eye as she released her final frustration and slammed the car door. As Ria buckled her seat belt, she felt lightheaded. She opened her bag, pulled out a bottle of water, and began to drink from it. She then threw her bag onto the passenger seat before she started the ignition. As Ria drove, she observed the dark blue sky. It was a calm, clear night. She turned on the radio, hoping that the music would change the atmosphere of her tense and emotional mind. She could not believe how Shawn had reacted. Just thinking about what he had said made her think of all the other arguments they'd had that week.

Ria approached Chanel's two-story, brick home and got out of her car feeling very tearful and overwhelmed. She lifted up the brass knocker and tapped it twice on the door.

Ria was proud of her big sister's success. Chanel was a devoted Christian and a dedicated church member. She was happily married to a successful associate minister who loved the pants off of her, literally. They had problems every now and then, but they always got through it. Chanel gave her life to Christ when she was almost murdered by a former abusive boyfriend ten years ago. She prayed to God that if he got her out of the relationship, she would devote her life completely to God. The pain she suffered at the hands of her ex led her to set up her own charity to help women who were experiencing domestic violence.

As Chanel opened her door, she was pleasantly surprised to see her little sister standing there. A closer look at Ria, however, revealed a distraught expression in the depths of her sister's eyes.

"Ri, what's up, what's happened?" Chanel asked.

"You have no idea..."

Ria walked straight through the hallway and into the sitting area. She flopped down on the cream leather couch and dropped her bag to the floor. Ria blurted out in one breath, "I'm so fed up, Chan, for once in my life I have an opportunity to go for my dreams, and it's like I have to put it on the back seat, and my heart is tearing up, I'm tired." Ria said.

"Ri, you must have known that relocating to New York was going to have an impact on your relationship," Chanel said softly. Though Ria never mentioned Shawn's name, Chanel knew her sister's angst came from her relationship. "You've been living in each other's pockets for over seven years, girl." Chanel said.

"I understand that, Chan. But the fact that I have devoted so much energy into this relationship, doesn't that stand for anything? Who was there when his mother died, waking up in the middle of the night to him crying? I went through the whole grieving process with him. Now when it's time for me to establish myself away from him, it's like the noose that he has around my neck gets tighter." Ria leaned her head back onto the couch, relieved to have some breathing space. As she wiped the tears from her eyes, she exhaled.

"The one thing I know, Ri, is that Shawn really does love you and maybe he's taking the news a bit hard. Give him some time. He's still probably mourning the loss of his mother, and he feels that he's losing you, too. Remember it was only a year ago that it all happened." Chanel said.

"I love Shawn. You know I do. But maybe I've loved him too much and forgot about myself. I don't think he realizes how much I even love him." Just as Ria was going to start another sentence, Chanel's daughter Desiree came skipping out of the kitchen.

"Hello, Aunty Ria, what's the matter?" she asked with her little arms open.

"Hi, baby," Ria said, hugging Desiree. "I'm okay. How is my favorite niece?"

"I'm good. I just had my hot chocolate. Why are you crying aunty?" Desiree wiped Ria's face with her little fingers.

"Why are you down here?" Chanel asked sharply. "You need to be in your bed, girl. It's past eight o'clock—way past your bedtime."

"I heard Aunty Ria's voice, so I wanted to see her." Desiree said.

"Okay, now you've seen her, you can go back to bed." Chanel said.

"Oh, Mom…"

"Goodnight, Desiree." Chanel said.

"Goodnight, baby. I'll come and see you again and take you to the park," Ria said while hugging Desiree and giving her a kiss on her forehead.

Ria watched Desiree skipped up the stairs with such freedom, she only wished she could returned to that place of liberty. Chanel looked at Ria from head to toe with concern. "Have you been eating? You don't look so good. You look like you've lost a few pounds."

"I've been overworked and overstressed these couple of months. There's been so much arguing between Shawn and me that I guess it's taking a toll on my body."

Chanel moved from her original seat and sat closer to Ria. She then looked at her curiously. "You're not pregnant, are you?" Chanel said cautiously. "Mom said she dreamt of fish, and I know it's not me." Chanel said.

"Mom's always having those superstitious dreams." Ria hesitated. "Even though Shawn would love for us to have a baby. But that's not possible now." Ria looked down at her shoes as if they held the answers to her distress.

"Look, the only person that can help you now is God. He can direct you and bring peace to your storm. So let's pray about it and afterwards get some food. Everything will be all right." Ria looked up at her sister and nodded. "Okay, Chan. Thank you."

"For what?"

"For listening to my drama."

"Isn't that what big sisters are for?"

Chanel grabbed a couple of Kleenex tissues from off the coffee table and wiped the rest of Ria's tears from her face.

*****

It was late when Ria returned from Chanel's house. Chanel always knew how to encourage her in her time of need. She pondered on a Bible verse Chanel had paraphrased to her: "God in his own time will make all things beautiful." She continued to meditate on those words and tried to dismiss the thought of her actually being pregnant.

Ria pulled into her driveway, killed the ignition, and remained seated in the car, thoughtfully tapping her fingers against the steering wheel. The whole idea of her being pregnant out of wedlock was one of Ria's biggest fears—thanks to her mother. She always expected Ria to fall down that road of life of single motherhood.

"You are just like your father, useless. He couldn't grab a peg if it was on his nose," Ria's mother would say. "You'll probably end up pregnant and by yourself." The words stayed with Ria as she sat in her car.

She gripped the steering wheel, this time to help the tension she was feeling. It was now almost midnight, and the car radio was on a smooth jazz station. Ria sat back and allowed the bass and saxophone to soothe her ears. The melody put Ria's soul at ease. As the song finished, Ria looked up at her apartment to see whether there were any lights on. The lights were off, so Ria assumed that Shawn was asleep.

Ria rubbed her churning stomach as she walked up her apartment steps. What if her mother was right? What would she do? Having to exchange the job of her dreams for being barefoot and pregnant did not seem like a good deal at all. Any extra pressure on her and Shawn's relationship now seemed crucial in breaking them apart. A break now seemed to be the better option than a baby. Once again, Ria pushed the thought from her mind as she carefully opened her front door.

Shawn was already in bed asleep when Ria entered their bedroom. She was relieved and made every effort not to wake him. The moonlight peeked through the curtains, allowing her to see what she had to do to prepare herself for bed. As she looked at Shawn, the moonlight highlighted his chiseled profile. It was hard for her to stay mad at him when she knew his heart behind all the arguing and fussing. She glanced at Shawn as she undressed and wondered what their child would look like. She hated herself for even thinking it, but she could not help but imagine her smile and his eyes in a miniature version. She smiled and then pushed the thought out of her mind again. Ria took a white towel from the cupboard and walked off naked into their bathroom. She ensured that the bathroom door was firmly shut before she turned on the light.

Just before stepping into the shower, she turned on Shawn's bathroom radio and tuned the dial until she found her jazz station. This time, the melody was a collection of Congo drums and a piano fused together with harmonized soul vocals. As the shower rain hit her skin, the scent of her ginger and nutmeg shower gel mixed with the steam gradually began to relax her. After a while Ria stepped out of the shower, took the towel which she hung over the shower door, and began to dry herself off. She then opened her mango body butter and massaged the cream into her skin. Exhausted, Ria re-entered their bedroom and readied herself for a goodnight sleep. She put on one of Shawn's old Nike T-shirts and crawled onto the bed behind him. He stirred slightly as the sweet smelling fragrance passed his nose. He turned toward her and stroked her face with his hand.

"I'm sorry for acting like a jerk earlier. I am happy that you got the job. You deserve it, and I would not want to hold you back from your dreams." Shawn said. Ria stroked Shawn's head and felt her body go weak in his arms. She hated any man having this power over her. But she loved this man that had been arguing with her for the past two months. He was all she knew sexually and emotionally. It was times like this, nothing else could compare to this feeling she felt for him. She could see them lasting forever. She knew him more than he knew himself.

Over the seven years that they had been together, they had both explored and endured each other's weaknesses, fears, and dreams. Having to give up this for a while seemed like a mistake now.

"Shawn, I love you, and there is no other man that can take your place."

"Not even a rich New Yorker that can give you the world?" He said.

"I don't need to be given the world before I'm satisfied." She said.

"Not even Denzel?"

"No silly, of course not…" Ria chuckled. "And anyway, he's a bit old now. He wouldn't be able to handle a young thang like me."

They both chuckled before Ria looked at Shawn in the half-moonlit room, and her face turned solemn. "Are we going to survive this, Shawn?" Short silence extended before Shawn replied, "I don't know, baby. I really don't know." Ria watched the steam disintegrate out of the en-suite bathroom. The sweet scent of her shower gel kissed the atmosphere of their room, but was unable to sweeten the uncertainly of their future.

Chapter Three

*R*ia pushed the box of Christmas decorations out of the hall closet in an attempt to grab her small weekend bag she used for travelling.

"Are you going to put them up before you go?" Ria's friend Cissy asked from Ria's bedroom which was opposite the closet.

"I don't know. I haven't given it much thought. I've been so occupied, I haven't even thought about Christmas. Anyway I really don't have time for that."

Ria grabbed her weekend bag and placed her face wipes into it in preparation for her flight to New York the next day. It all seemed surreal to her as everything happened to move so quickly. It still had not soaked in that she was moving to New York. Every time she thought about it, her tummy turned with anxiety. Ria still had not seen her period, and a slight panic pinched her from time to time. The distance between her and Shawn was still evident, which made her not even want to deal with finding out whether she was pregnant or not.

Even though she was weak, it took all she had to hold herself together. She had to be strong and focus on the next chapter she was entering. Ria's boss, James, had arranged her accommodation so that she could focus on settling in and get into her new position. Ria had wished that she could at least spend Christmas at home with Shawn, but everything was now set and she felt very fortunate for the opportunity and did not want to advantage.

Ria returned to her bedroom and continued packing the last few items of clothing into her suitcase. Ria placed a blue sweater and a pile of boxer shorts into her suitcase, she could feel eyes peering into her back. She turned and faced Cissy.

"Girl, what are you doing?" Cissy asked bewildered. Ria looked down at her suitcase. "I did not even realize... I'm so used to..." Ria sighed and placed the items back onto the bed. It was now creeping up on Ria how much she had built her life around Shawn; they were almost entwined. Cissy rolled her eyes up to the ceiling and loosened her black shawl, which revealed her apple shape. Cissy was a jazz singer and a little older than the rest of Ria's close friends. At thirty-eight, Cissy had the house, car, and a good man at home. Ria always looked up to Cissy as her mentor.

"It's getting hot in here," do you mind if I open the window?" Cissy said.

Ria nodded and Cissy walked over to the window and pulled it open. Immediately a cool breeze entered into the room, allowing Cissy's dreadlocks to move slightly. Cissy picked up one of Ria's clips and grasped her long locks tinted with light brown tips into one.

"You know," Ria said, "you are really beginning to remind me of India Arie every time I see you."

"India Arie with a big butt I suppose, anyway I was here before Miss Arie came on the scene."

Ria and Cissy turned toward the en-suite bathroom door where their girlfriend Tandra emerged rubbing her stomach.

"Oh boy, you would have thought after three kids those menstrual pains would have stopped by now," Tandra said, while she flopped down on Ria's bed and lay on her back. Tandra had a lot of history with men and had lost hope in ever getting married. She had three kids with three different men whom she assumed were the fathers.

"It's because you don't eat. Your hair is as thin as your waist." Cissy said, staring at Tandra.

"This is California. People don't eat here. Besides, it's not my fault that I'm a natural size six." Tandra said.

"A natural fool if you ask me," Cissy responded.

Tandra was used to Cissy's straight talking. She turned from

Cissy's gaze and turned on her side toward where Ria was kneeling down. Ria tried to not take notice of them both and decided to concentrate on getting herself prepared for her move.

"Girl, can you believe you're going to New York?" Cissy asked. "You better take some thick sweaters. It gets cold out there especially in winter." Cissy pulled the door of Ria's closet open and peered inside its half-empty contents. "With that big paycheck you'll be getting, you don't need all these raggedy old clothes." Cissy said.

"Oh, so now you can tell me that my clothes are raggedy? Is that what you thought when I was wearing them?" Ria laughed.

"No, baby, I was just saying that..."

"It's all right, no need to explain, because I'm gonna hook myself up with a new closet for my new position," Ria said while trying to shake her hips.

"Hope you don't go looking too cute. Remember you will still have a man back here." Cissy said.

Ria laughed nervously as she struggled to close her red suitcase.

Tandra laid quietly on her side, waiting for her period pain to subside.

"Got any Advil, Ria? I need about six right now."

Ria reached over to her bedside cabinet and took a pack out and chucked it to Tandra on the bed.

"You better take two. I haven't got time to take anyone to the hospital today."

Cissy was observing Ria. She could read through Ria's façade, and she looked at her questionably. She could tell that Ria had something heavy on her mind.

"So you and Shawn are settling to have a long distance relationship then?" Cissy asked while Tandra swallowed the two tablets and looked at Ria for a response.

"I could come over for the holidays, and he can come over as well..." Ria began, but Cissy cut her off.

"Are you sure that is going to work?" Cissy asked with a frown. You're leaving a good man behind who treasures you and who has been faithful to you. It's not too late to change your mind."

"Change my mind! Are you crazy? I've made my decision, and I'm sticking with it, okay?" Ria snapped. It was already hard enough for her. She was already convincing herself every time she placed an item of clothing into her suitcase.

"That fine man of yours will be snatched up as quickly as you get on the plane, honey. With all these fast LA girls!" Tandra said, adding wood to the fire.

Cissy rolled her eyes as Ria shook her head at Tandra's remark; she marched over to the bathroom to fetch her toiletry bag.

"The thing is you are getting older and you have no children. If you end a seven-year relationship with the man you have grown with, you're gonna have to start all over again," Cissy stated firmly. "Once you've found a good man, you should never let him go."

"Cissy! You are starting to sound like my mother," Ria said from inside the en-suite bathroom.

As Ria returned from the bathroom, she slightly stepped back as though she had lost her balance.

"You alright, Ri?" Cissy asked.

"All this moving and talking has been stressing me out a little." Ria said.

"Maybe you need some rest. Do you want me to call Shawn?" Tandra asked.

"No, no, there's no need for that. I probably just need some rest," Ria said, hoping that they would leave.

Cissy caught the hint, got up from the bed, and swung her black shawl around her shoulders.

"Come on, Tandra," she whispered. "Let's leave Miss New York alone so she can get some rest." She kissed Ria on the cheek. "I'll call you later tonight. There's more to this than I thought." Cissy said.

"Girl, all the best, and don't try to forget me," Tandra said, pulling Ria into a hug. "You know me and the kids will be coming over for the holidays."

"You and your rug rats are welcomed anytime once I'm settled, T."

As Cissy and Tandra hustled out the room waving goodbye, Ria dropped back on her bed and hummed to Boys II Men's Motown Philly, which was playing in the background. As she closed her eyes, Shawn entered the room with a bouquet of a dozen roses.

"Are they for me?" she asked, her face beaming as she sat upright.

Shawn reviewed the room and the open suitcases, then he handed the bouquet of flowers to her. As Ria hugged him, he embraced her firmly in his arms and kissed the side of her neck. The distance he had been trying to portray was coming back to bite him. His body was yearning for her. Just the thought of her being absent from him was already breaking his heart. He took the flowers back from her hand and threw them by Ria's suitcases. He wanted more than to kiss her neck.

Shawn did not want to let Ria out of his life; his mother was gone and Ria was all he had to be his back bone when things got tough. If he could show her how much he loved her, maybe she would change her mind. As they embraced in a passionate kiss, his hands moved down to unbutton her jeans. Shawn managed to unbutton the first button when Ria pulled away. He looked at her as she released herself from his embrace, denting his ego. Shawn tried to search Ria's eyes for a reason, but she refused to look at him.

"I-I still got loads to do and these beautiful flowers need to go in some water," Ria said as she nervously left the arms of Shawn and went to pick up the flowers. Shawn wanted to say more, but Ria's reaction was making it hard for him to be open. Ria was the only person he could be weak with, and he found strength in that. In Ria he saw his wife to be and the future mother of their children. He did not want to be selfish and force her into abandoning her dreams for his.

"Okay well at least come with me. We're gonna do something a little different for lunch today." Shawn said.

"Oh, but I'm so tired, Shawn."

"It won't take long, I promise you. Come on, you won't have to do a thing. Anyway, I have everything prepared for today so..."

"You...have something prepared? This should be interesting."

Ria was surprised. Over the past few weeks, she had wondered whether he was ever going to acknowledge her at all on her last days with him. Ria slipped on her flip-flops with expectation as they both headed out to the car. She began to grow with excitement and the tiredness withered away. She looped her hands with Shawn's and kissed him on the cheek. Shawn opened the car door and waited for Ria to slip onto her seat. As Ria looked into Shawn's eyes, she could tell that his mind was occupied.

As they both settled into opposite sides of the car, Ria smelt the aroma of chicken. She turned her head toward the back of the car to locate where the smell was coming from. As Shawn drove, she looked at his face, trying to read into his facial expression and thoughts. Shawn continued to remain focused on the road.

"Do you mind if I turn the radio on?" Ria asked.

"No, go ahead."

In the past few weeks, the radio had become Ria's best friend, especially the smooth jazz station. As she turned on the radio, she twisted the dial straight to the station.

"You seem to be listening to this station a lot lately."

"Yeah, it's nice and relaxing. You don't like it?"

"Urr, it's all right I suppose. It's a bit like elevator music."

"Elevator music?" Ria exaggerated a laugh in an attempt to change the awkwardness between them. "You aren't listening right. This is smooth jazz. Good quality music." Ria said.

"Sounds just like elevator music to me, put you straight to sleep. That's why you're so tired all the time. I've noticed any time you put that music on, within ten minutes you're sleeping, with your mouth open and everything. Knocks you right out." They both laughed.

"It relaxes me from stress. Am I drooling? A good sleep makes you drool, you know honey." Ria said.

"Baby, I saw you drooling so bad one time, I had to put a

bucket under your head. I thought you were gonna drown the whole apartment."

Ria laughed so much that tears began to stream from her eyes. The moment reminded her of when they were in college and used to tease each other.

"Really, at least I don't be snoring down the whole block. One time you were snoring so loud, I woke up and thought we were having an earthquake. The bed was shaking, the whole house was moving. I almost ran downstairs and hid under the table. But I'm not mad at you it's just the after-effect of my lovemaking, honey. I just thought I'd chip that in so you don't get it twisted." Ria said as she also laughed.

"You kinda getting good at this now, aren't you?" Shawn said at Ria quick comeback.

"I've learned from the best."

As they reached the beach and parked, Shawn went to the trunk and took out a picnic basket and a table cloth.

"Oh, so that's where that smell was coming from? What else you got in there?"

"You'll just have to wait and see."

They found a spot to settle, and Ria helped with the small picnic Shawn had laid out for her. He handed her the beach mat for them to sit on and placed the basket in the middle.

"This is nice, Shawn." She looked at him, waiting for a response, but he just smiled vaguely. Ria sighed and focused her attention on her surroundings. All the mixed signals Shawn was sending confused her. She looked at the waves of the ocean and wondered why God had them so free and full of beauty.

Ria also observed the bird's that flew in the sky; it had seemed that they were dancing with the clouds as though it was a game.

Soft music flowing from the little portable radio Shawn had brought with him freed her thoughts from the sky. She reached over to where it was. Shawn looked at her as she took it, smiled, and shook his head, already knowing what station she would tune into.

"As long as you don't sleep on me, you're allowed," he said.

As they sat on the beach mat, they both reached for the food. Ria observed the menu by picking each container up.

"What type of picnic is this? Where are the sandwiches?" Ria asked with amusement. Shawn grinned. "I got what you like but no sandwiches." They both dug into the fried chicken and rice, which was neatly organized in polythene containers.

The transparency of the ocean turned dark blue as the sun descended onto the horizon, turning the sky shades of yellow and orange. This blended into the soft jazz music playing from the portable radio. The Isley Brothers' "Living for the Lover in You" came on.

"Hmmm, this is my song. Let's dance." Ria reached a hand out to Shawn while licking the mayonnaise off her thumb from the potato salad. Shawn hesitantly accepted her invitation and held her hand as he got up. She drew him close to her, and Shawn, slightly embarrassed, looked around the beach to see if anyone was watching them.

"This is really something different, Shawn—a picnic and a dance on the beach."

They moved slowly, grooving to the jam that was sweetening the mood. Ria knew Shawn was not the type to dance in public. After she pulled away from his advances earlier on, she could feel that distance returning. As the song came to an end, Shawn loosened his grip on her waist.

"Ria, we need to talk."

"Shawn, do we have to? I really don't want to spoil a good evening. I haven't got the strength to argue with you tonight." Ria said softly.

"No, we are not gonna argue. I promise."

"All right. What is it?" Ria folded her arms defensively.

"We have been together for seven years now. I've loved each and every moment of it, the good times and the bad times..."

Ria's excitement grew.

Is he going to propose? Ria thought as she unfolded her arms and took his hand in hers and widened her eyes.

"... I love you and you'll always be in my heart. There will be

no other woman that could or will take that residence. As you are moving to New York, I have been thinking a lot about us and our relationship and the changes it will make to our lives, and I think we should..."

Ria looked deep into Shawn's eyes as she held her breath in anticipation, waiting for him to say the words.

"...separate."

Ria's heart felt like it had dropped to her feet, and Shawn had kicked it into the ocean.

"You want to separate? I don't understand. You want to throw away seven years just like that, Shawn?" Ria dropped Shawn's hand like a hot rod and stepped back from him and put her hand to her forehead.

"I think it will be best for both of us. There's no point kidding ourselves, Ria."

"What do you mean best for us? Maybe it's best for you. I have been close to a wife to you, Shawn, with no ring, no commitment from you. I have stood by you and now, when I want to chase my dream, it's like you can't handle it." Ria turned her back and faced the sea. Silence stretched between them.

Shawn thought of the engagement ring he had bought for Ria six months ago. He had been waiting for the perfect moment to present it to her.

"Tell me something," Shawn said. "If we were married, would that have changed your mind about taking the position?"

Ria turned her head to the side as the descending sun enhanced her profile. "What are you talking about?"

"If you were my wife, would you stay?" He said helplessly.

"No, Shawn, I would not have stayed. I still would have expected you to support me."

Shawn returned to the beach mat and began to pack up the picnic.

Ria bit her lip hard to stop herself from crying. She did not want Shawn to see the tears that flowed down her face. The light ocean breeze helped evaporate the tears of loss that she felt. She had given Shawn her heart, body, and soul and now, it was as if

those parts were physically absent from her.

*****

During the silent drive back home, Ria wondered why Shawn would want to break up with her. Did he have another woman? Somehow that reasoning did not sit well with her conscience. Shawn was not the cheating type, and he steered away from any type of behavior that resembled his father.

The thought of her being pregnant now pinched her thoughts again. Being a single mother was Ria's worst nightmare. How could she tell Shawn now that there could be a possibility of her being pregnant? She knew that he would force her to stay if she even hinted that she was pregnant, and she was not ready to fight that fight. Ria's mind flew with busy thoughts she leaned her head on the window.

She cut her eye at Shawn before she returned her attention back on the window. Ria really wanted to pop him on the side of his head, but she decided to grind her teeth together instead. She knew he hated that. Shawn looked at her, but she took no notice of him and continued to look at the road ahead of her. She now felt a slight relief that she was going to New York. Away from all the drama she was contending with.

He better not even think about having no goodbye sex tonight, Ria thought. In fact, I dare him to even come and try. It would give me a reason to really pop him in his mouth. Ria cut her eye at Shawn again.

Chapter Four

S hawn looked up at the night blue sky, then glanced at his watch. It was a quarter to ten. As they walked into their apartment, Shawn noticed the new message light blinking on the phone. He waited first for Ria to pass him, then he picked up the receiver and followed the automated voice to retrieve the messages. The first message was from Cissy, asking Ria to call her back. Shawn rolled his eyes. As he continued to listen, the second message tweaked his ears.

"This is a message for Shawn Matthews. This is Coach Wagner from the Stallions…" Shawn looked over his shoulder to ensure Ria was not nearby.

"I was at one of your games the other day and wanted to know if you would like to come over to work for us. Anyway, come down to the office about 8:30 tomorrow morning, so we can talk business with Don Howard. Any problems, call me." Shawn's jaw dropped; he moved his hands over his face and then down to his mouth before he returned the receiver to the cradle. Shawn had been playing as a quarterback for the Red Lions. He often felt that he could do better, but it paid the bills. Since his mother died of cancer, he had lost all hope in achieving his dream in playing for the NFL.

The Stallions were one of the top five teams in the country. Shawn grabbed the notepad that was by the phone and wrote down the time. He grunted as he realized that the appointment clashed with Ria's flight time.

As Ria passed him again, entering into the kitchen, Shawn went upstairs to their bedroom and called his brother Kenny on his cell.

"Kenny, it's Shawn."

"Yeah man, what's up?"

"I've been called to have a meeting with the Stallion's coach tomorrow morning, and it clashes with Ria's flight. I told her I would drop her off, but I can't now."

"You got called by the Stallions? That's great news. Congratulations."

"Well, let's wait and see what happens first."

"I'm very happy for you. Man, you deserve it. The only thing I'm not convinced about is that girlfriend of yours. You know how sista's act when brothers get into the money. She will be trying to claim half of everything you have. Especially that Miss Independent leaving you to pursue her career in New York. Have you ditched her yet?"

"I never ditched her, Kenny. We both ended it. I couldn't see the point of us continuing to have a relationship when she is halfway across the country."

"Good man. I'm glad you got yourself out of that noose. So, so…how did she take it?" Kenny said inquisitively.

"Not too well, I suppose. Anyway, I really don't want to get into it right now." Shawn said.

"All right, I'll take her to the airport. I'll do it for you, but she better not come with no mood; otherwise, she'll find herself on the freeway hitchhiking to New York." Kenny said.

"Look, Kenny, whether she comes with an attitude or not, I want you to take her there safely."

"All right, all right, I'm just messing, man. Why you got to be so serious? She'll be all right. It seems she still got you whipped, though."

"No, it's love. Feelings just don't go like that, Kenny. So get here at 7:15 at the latest. Her flight leaves at a quarter to ten, and it's gonna take at least an hour for you to drive to LAX and give her enough time to check in."

"No problem, I'll be there. Promise. Does she know that you're not taking her to the airport?"

"No, not yet. I just wanted to check with you first. If she wild's out, I'll just pay for her to get a taxi." Shawn said.

"What? You gonna spend almost $100 on her just because she don't want to ride wid me? I can hear a whiplash now. Thank God you're out of that manipulation."

Shawn shook his head. One thing Shawn knew about his brother was that he was never serious, which was a good and bad thing. "Look I just want to leave things on a good note. Life is just too short."

"All right man, it's your money. Anyway, I'll be there at quarter after seven, unless you tell me otherwise." Kenny said.

"Thanks, Kenny. Talk to you later."

As Shawn ended the call, he stood there in his bedroom. How was he going to tell Ria that he couldn't drop her off at the airport? Just before he could prepare his reason, Ria walked into their bedroom. She looked at him as if to wonder why he was standing in the middle of the room.

Shawn hesitated before speaking. "Something's come up and I can't take you to the airport tomorrow, so Kenny is going to take you there. If you're not comfortable with that, I'll call you a taxi. He's going to pick you up at seven fifteen."

"Hell no! You know that I don't get on with that sorry excuse for a man." Ria said.

"That's a bit harsh. That's my brother you're talking about," Shawn said calmly.

"Oh please, even you know he's good for nothing and you've asked him to drop me to the airport?"

"He has had a tough life. It's not his fault that his life is the way it is."

"Please don't make me laugh, Shawn. Are you talking about that one time when you were young? You need to stop glossing over your brother's issues and allowing him to use the past as an excuse to be an ass now."

Shawn sighed. He did not want another argument spanning out of control. "Look, just give him a chance that's all I'm asking." Shawn said.

"Whatever," Ria said dismissively. Shawn stared at Ria as she struggled to pull her suitcase into the hallway. He went over to help her.

"Don't worry about it. I'm fine. I can handle my business. I'm gonna have to learn sooner or later."

"Ria, look, I still love you, but we…"

"You better take the spare duvet out of the closet now because I'll be going to bed soon and I don't want to be disturbed." Ria snapped.

Ria sprinted past him, sharply leaving a cool breeze in her walk. He made his way to the living room and stretched out his tall frame on the couch. He could hear Ria moving around the apartment and sighed. It was a shame, he thought. Everything they had built and accomplished had been torn down. There wasn't even a child between them to show what they once had. Shawn often spoke to Ria about starting a family, but Ria did not seem fond of the idea and always told him that it was not the right time. After losing his mother, Shawn's desire to have children increased, and Ria was the only woman who he wanted to be the mother of his children.

A picture on the mantelpiece caught his attention. He focused on the photograph of Ria and him smiling as though they were the only lovers in the world. He got up, walked over to the mantel, and picked up the picture. In his heart, he wished tonight was the night he had proposed to her, and that they were going to enter the next chapter of their lives as husband and wife, instead of separate paths. *Starting off new will probably be the best for both of us*, Shawn thought as he placed the picture back in its original position. He walked back to the couch and stretched himself out again. His mind meditated on his mother; he was still struggling with her being gone. He needed her here with him, to comfort him and to fix the very thing that was breaking his heart.

It seemed that now all he had left in life was his brother Kenny.

*****

While in the shower, Ria thought about her day. She allowed the shower steam to ease her of her troubling thoughts. But the steam wasn't working. Kenny was dropping her off. He was not supposed to be the one seeing her off, wishing her, her last farewells.

Ria's body became tense over having to spend almost an hour in his company. She and Kenny were like oil and water. Shawn had a strong relationship with Kenny, and many times Ria had taken a second seat to Kenny.

As the water from the shower kissed her skin and she washed off the soap lather for the umpteenth time, Ria asked herself if she was making the right decision. Her mom advised her against taking the job. But Ria's mom was old fashioned in thinking and had held on to Ria's dad after he had cheated on her and had six kids outside the marriage. Knowing the behavior her mom had and the hurt she suffered over the years made Ria a very strong woman. She stepped out the bath, dried off with a towel, and wrapped her house coat around her body. Though she was hurting, Ria decided that she would not leave Shawn on this note.

She regretted chucking him out onto the sofa. Somehow, deep down inside, she knew that Shawn loved her and probably needed time to take it all in.

Ria crept down the dark stairs and stood by the doorway of the sitting room. There, she saw Shawn stretched out on his back on the couch, sleeping. She walked toward him, bent down, and awakened him with a gentle kiss on his lips.

"We just cannot leave things like this. I love you too much," Ria whispered.

Shawn did not speak; he just drew Ria close and held her in his arms. He stroked her shoulder as she embraced him and they lay there before commencing to their bedroom.

Chapter Five

*R*ia stirred out of her sleep, drained from the night before. She had gotten up twice that morning to vomit. She stretched her hand onto the empty side of the bed. Elated by Shawn's absence, she rolled onto her belly and took a few moments to be still in the silence that surrounded her. Only then did she remembered Shawn telling her that something had come up, but she did not think he would leave before she woke up. Ria had not even heard him go out, which she thought was quite strange.

Maybe he's going to pop up at the airport, she thought. Just as she pushed herself up onto her elbows, her house phone rang. Her voice was croaky as she said, "Hello, Ria speaking."

"Hi Ri, where were you last night? I tried calling you. I even left a message. Is everything all right?"

"Well, yes and no, Cissy. In a sentence, I'll say it like this: I will be leaving LA with no strings attached."

"I don't understand."

"Shawn broke up with me yesterday."

"Huh? Why? I mean, what happened? Were you guys arguing again?"

"No. He took me out after you guys left and told me that there was no point of us continuing a relationship." Ria said.

"How do you feel about that?" Cissy said.

"To tell you the truth, Cissy, I really can't deal with it right now. I'm just trying to stay focused. We kind of left things on a good note, anyway," Ria said, trying to sound optimistic.

"Just what have you got yourself into? Are you sure you're making the right choice?"

"Well I've already made it now, and as the saying goes, I've made my bed, so I have to lay in it."

Ria knew that Cissy didn't mean any harm, but she was starting to get fed up with the resistance she was receiving from her decision to relocate to New York. She already had her doubts, and with everyone second-guessing her decision, it only made her feel even more uneasy about the whole thing. Never in a million years did she think that she would be facing this situation. What made it even worse was the fact that Shawn had broken the relationship, making Ria feel that she had nothing to lose. She did not want to be in a position where she stayed and lived in resentment.

"Anyway, Cissy, I've got to get myself together. Kenny's coming to pick me up in an hour."

"Why is Kenny picking you up? Where's Shawn?"

"He's out. He said he had something to do."

"I'm shocked. Maybe he'll surprise you at the airport," Cissy said, trying to erase the sullen tone she heard in Ria's voice.

"Maybe and maybe not." Ria said.

"Well I guess we'll see you in February for your birthday?" Cissy said.

"I'm not sure. I might just keep my head down for Christmas and my birthday. Get myself settled out there for a few months before I visit. If anything I'll hang out with James."

"Hmm James, huh? If I did not know you well, I swear you two had a thing going on."

"Don't even go there," Ria said.

They both chuckled. "Anyway I originally called you for two things: to wish my baby all the best in New York and tell you how much I'm gonna really miss you, and I know it seems that you are making a huge sacrifice, but it will be all worth it in the end."

"Thank you, Cissy. I really appreciate that. I'm gonna really really miss you to bits. You better come and visit me."

"I will, honey. Call me when you get there, just so I know you made it there safe." Cissy said.

"Talk to you later."

Ria looked at the time and realized that she had to get herself ready for her flight. All of her stuff was packed, and she had laid out her clothes for that day the night before. Even though Shawn had left without a sound, she knew that they had ended the night on a better note. So if she did not see him at the airport, she would call him when she got to New York.

Ria hustled to the bathroom and quickly washed herself and put on her clothes. Though she was flying business class, Ria decided to wear a black jogging suit. It was a long flight, and she wanted to be as comfortable as possible. As she placed her address details and contact number on the mantel piece, she saw an envelope with her name on it. She knew it had to be from Shawn. She smiled and placed it in her bag.

After Ria had finished combing her hair and putting on her lip gloss, she suddenly found herself craving toast and jelly. She held her hungry stomach, went over to the fridge, and fixed what her stomach suddenly desired. As the smell of heated bread filled the kitchen, she heard a car pull up outside, and she peeped through the kitchen window. Kenny's black Chrysler pulled into the driveway.

"God give me strength to deal with this fool," she said with annoyance.

The intercom buzzed and Ria's toast popped up at the same time. Ria decided that she would deal with her toast first. She quickly buttered it, stuffed a piece of toast in her mouth, and chewed with reverence. The taste of the butter on the bread made Ria's eyes roll with satisfaction. *Hmm, that is just too good.* Ria walked over to the door with the remaining piece of toast in her hand and unlocked the door.

As Kenny entered into the hallway, he looked at Ria holding the piece of toast in her hand. She gave him a fake smile.

"Morning Kenneth," Ria said sarcastically.

"Hey Ria."

"I've got most of the suitcases upstairs and another one in the sitting room, which also needs to be taken down to the car. I hope you have made room in your car." Ria commanded.

Kenny looked at Ria and shook his head with a smile.

"What? What's the problem, Kenneth?"

"I can see why Shawn ditched you. I'm sure he couldn't handle all that nagging and ordering you do."

"Excuse me? What exactly are you talking about?" Ria turned to give Kenny her full attention.

"Don't hate. I'm just stating a fact, that's all. He couldn't handle it."

"You know nothing about our relationship, so don't even think about going there today." Ria said.

"I'm only going by what he told me. Don't shoot the messenger."

Ria was taken aback by Kenny's comment, and she wasn't sure about the truthfulness of his statements. Kenny and Shawn were close. Maybe he knew some things that she did not.

"I'll tell you what, Kenneth, I'll call for a taxi. I really cannot get into this with you. I truly don't have the strength to deal with your trash. I'm sure you're over the moon that Shawn and I have split up." Ria walked over to the phone to call a taxi.

"Hey now, let me explain, baby." Kenny walked over to Ria as she held the phone in mid-air, waiting for his explanation. "Shawn doesn't know how to treat and keep a woman like you. You need a man that will put you in your place."

"Oh, is that right?"

"Why you always want to fight with me, baby girl? Do you have a little crush on me or something?" Kenny said.

Ria laughed. "Oh, please. You are such a character, Kenneth, you really are."

"That's all right, though. We could do a little long distance thing if you like. You know, I fell in love with you the moment I saw you. I was mad when Shawn told me that you two were an item. So now that that's in the open, we can do our thing, right? Shawn don't need to know." Kenny said.

Ria stared at Kenny. "You cannot be serious. Hold on a

minute, you actually are…" Ria threw a hand on her hip. "Let me break this down to you, schizophrenic fool. There is and never will be anything between me and you. The fact that you would even consider your brother's girlfriend confirms everything that I have ever thought of you. And you will never be or become half the man Shawn was to me."

Ria went to dial the taxi again.

"You stupid chicken head, you really think Shawn loved you? And that he was devoted to you? Did he tell you that he got picked up by the Stallions?"

Ria stood there in silence, slightly stunned by Kenny's announcement.

"That's why he dumped you. He knew that he was getting a million dollar contract. He got tired of you, yeah tired of the same ol' thang he was getting every night."

Ria's breathing became heavy, and her mind raced with confusion. Why hadn't Shawn told her about the Stallions? She opened her mouth, tried to say something, but found it hard to speak. Somehow, what Kenny was saying to her was making sense. All of the strange behavior and arguments started to add up. Kenny's smile was devilish.

"That's where he is now, signing the contract."

"You know what, Kenny, maybe you're right about Shawn getting the contract, and I am happy for him. But the only thing that makes me sad about this whole situation is that he has a brother that would stab him in the back by chasing after someone he truly loves. And you know something else? At least I can stand and say that I have been a part of Shawn's success. As for you, Kenneth Matthews, you have only dragged him down with your drunk ass attitude."

Kenny gave Ria a dirty look from head to toe before he marched out and slammed the door behind him. Ria jumped as the door closed, then answered the young lady on the phone.

"Hello, yes, may I have a taxi to LAX airport… from 64 Cherry Wood Drive, Van Nays East…thank you, how much will that be? That's fine."

After hanging up the phone, Ria stood, stunned, still not believing what she had encountered with Kenny. She felt sick to her stomach that Kenny even imagined being with her. It hurt her to think that Kenny would do such a thing to his brother. Ria thought back to when they all used to hang out together. She could not believe that Kenny had feelings for her. Ria pushed it out her mind. Going to New York now, after that revelation, made her feel even better. She could not wait to get there and start fresh.

Chapter Six

I t had been a long night for Shawn; his mind had been busy thinking about the recent events. Leaving Ria while she was sleeping that morning was painful. He was gutted that he could not see her off at the airport, but he also could not pass up this opportunity. To him Ria demonstrated fierceness in achieving her goal, something he now had to adapt to.

Shawn parked the car, got out, and quickly checked his reflection in the door windows. He was wearing an all-black suit, and he had left the first two buttons of his shirt open to expose his athletic neck. He walked to the entrance of the Stallions' building and strode casually toward the reception desk.

An attractive white lady with honey blonde hair sat in front of a computer, her fingers moving with expertise over the keyboard. When she saw him, her fingers paused in their typing.

"Hello sir, how can I help you?" A smile touched her lips as she eyed Shawn's muscular physique.

"Hi, I'm here to see Coach Wagner. My name is Shawn Matthews."

"Hmm, Shawn Matthews." The receptionist leaned closer to Shawn. "Coach Wagner has been talking a lot about you."

"Oh really now? I hope it's all good things," Shawn said flirtatiously. They both chuckled.

"Believe me, it's all good things. Please take the elevator to the fifth floor, and it's the first office on your right. He's expecting you."

"Thanks."

As he turned toward the elevator, he felt the eyes of the receptionist piercing through his back. *Is she checking me out?* Shawn wondered.

He turned around and sure enough, she was. Shawn smiled and waited for the elevator doors to close. It had been a long time since Shawn had looked at another woman besides Ria. She was all he was interested in. He had plenty of opportunities to play away from home, but he did not see the sense in hurting someone he loved in that way.

As the elevator doors closed, he pressed the number five button and checked his watch. Ria was probably on the plane now, heading out to New York. It suddenly dawned on him that he was single again after seven years. Shawn collected his thoughts quickly as the doors reopened.

*****

During her flight, it was hard for Ria to sleep. She kept herself occupied by watching the movies and cartoons that were on. As she searched through her bag for a pen to do a crossword puzzle, she saw the pregnancy test that she had bought at the airport pharmacy. Over the past couple of months, she could feel her body going through changes she could not understand.

Ria took a deep breath while pushing the pregnancy test deeper into her bag and continued her search. Instead of a pen, her fingers brushed against the forgotten letter from Shawn. Should she open it, or just throw it away? He was a grown man. Whatever he wanted to say should have been said to her face. Ria held the envelope in her hand for a few seconds before she opened it. As she tore open the top of the envelope, anxiety crept into her belly. She unfolded the handwritten letter and read.

My best friend, my strength, and my lover. Leaving you this morning, knowing that you weren't coming back was the hardest thing I could come to terms with. What can I say but I love you, and I always will.

Shawn

Inside the envelope rested $1000 and a platinum diamond ring.

"Oh my goodness," Ria whispered. She held the letter to her chest. She lay back into her seat and closed her eyes as tears began to fall. She turned to face her small window and observed the clouds which looked like a thick white blanket below the plane. A flow of regret washed over her. Now, she felt like she was in the wrong place, and all she wanted to do was go home. It finally hit her that the man she loved was no longer in her life. Being alone was something that she had not considered in her plan to achieve her dream. Throughout her life, it always seemed that Shawn was there. Ria continued to stare out her window until her eyes felt heavy, and she finally fell asleep.

"Excuse me, Miss Jackson. We have landed. Do you need any assistance in getting to the airport lounge?"

Ria awoke to a friendly-faced flight attendant peering into her face. "Oh no, I'm okay, thank you."

Ria stretched her arms and yawned. It had been some of the best sleep she'd had in a long time. "I will need some help, though, with my luggage."

"Don't worry. There will be a concierge service available. Just let them know at the lounge."

"Oh thank you."

Ria had never experienced such service before. She was impressed. As she walked out of the airplane, she realized that she was walking through a different door to what she would normally go through on coach. She walked through a door with the other members of her cabin class and was greeted and told to take a seat. Before long, she heard her name being called. She stood and walked over to the gentleman who was standing with her luggage. "Hello, Miss Jackson. My name is Ricasso, and I will be assisting you with your luggage."

"Thank you." Ria said.

"Please follow me. We have a car ready to take you to your destination."

Ria nodded. She could get used to service like this.

After seeing Ricasso struggle to lift her suitcases into the car with its black-tinted windows, Ria gave the gentleman a ten dollar tip. She glanced around her surroundings before entering the car.

As the driver cruised from the airport to her place of residence, a little excitement and fear ran through Ria's body. She felt slightly refreshed after her nap on the plane. Her body, though rested, still felt drained…more mentally than physically. It was if she was walking with only half of her body. Right then and there, she decided that she would not allow herself to go into a love-sick, brokenhearted mode. As the car stopped at the traffic light, she took instruction from a billboard she saw: 'Life starts when you start loving it.' Ria managed to encourage herself, and she smiled as she glanced at the new land she had stepped into. The multicolored lights and Christmas decorations illuminated the buildings.

New York was quite a contrast from LA. The tall gray buildings that Ria passed looked so intimidating, the weather was cool and wet, and everything seemed to synchronize with the color gray. Riding through Manhattan, she peeked through the window like an excited child. Everything looked so busy and occupied.

The taxi stopped outside a brightly lit apartment complex, and Ria took out her purse to pay the driver.

"No, madam, it's a part of the service. Would you like some help with your luggage?"

"Oh, I keep forgetting," Ria said, trying not to seem like a novice. The driver assisted her with unloading her suitcases and then placed them at the entrance.

"Thank you very much." Ria handed him a ten dollar tip, left her luggage at the entrance, and stepped inside the building.

The entrance of the apartment complex reminded her of a 5-star hotel, so clean and modern, with plants and clean cream carpets. She approached a tall, elderly black guy with a friendly face. He kind of reminded her of Danny Glover.

"Hello, my name is Ria Jackson. I'm supposed to be occupying an apartment here."

"Good evening, ma'am. You just leave your luggage out there. I will get someone to bring it up to you. Here are your keys to the apartment. It's number 16 on the third floor." He said.

Wow, Ria thought. "Thank you very much, sir."

She took her small vanity case and walked over to the elevator. Walking through the hallway, she admired the Picasso-style paintings on the wall that complemented the decor. Ria entered the mirrored elevator and pressed the number 3 button. When the elevator doors closed, she glared at her tired reflection. *I was walking around business class like this? Shame on me.* She said to herself.

She examined her face, and something about her countenance looked different, but she could not quite put her finger on it. Instead of worrying, Ria clasped her hands together in anticipation of what her apartment would look like. Her heart began to race as she exited the elevator. Her eyes glazed across the doors in search of her apartment number. She counted to herself, *Number 12, 13, 14, 15...there it is.*

When she opened the door, she poked her head around the door before it could fully open. A lavender aroma caressed her senses as her fingers searched for a light switch in the lowly lit hallway. Her fingers finally brushed against the little knob and she switched the lights on. Ria smiled. She could not believe what she was seeing. Christmas and her birthday had come early all wrapped up in one.

She entered the open plan living room and glanced at the glass coffee table and the huge window showing the view of Manhattan. The window was framed by huge, dark-chocolate, velvet curtains. The kitchen had black graphite worktops with a stainless steel cooker, oven, and deluxe fridge. The ceilings were high, revealing the brick in some areas. It was a stylish combination.

Ria searched for the master bedroom, and when she found it, her lips lifted in a satisfied smile. The room had a high King-sized bed, which was covered with a black fluffy comforter, along with big cream suede scatter cushions. The bed rested in the middle of the large bedroom, and it was adjacent to a wall of mirrors that opened up into a spacious closet full of compartments and hangers. On one side of the wall, opposite the bed, was a 42-inch, flat screen television.

A half-opened door attached another smaller room to the master bedroom. Ria pushed open the door and entered a lavish en-suite bathroom with a walk-in shower displaying sandy marble tiles. The sink matched the shower's décor with its stylish, polished taps. Returning to the hallway, she eased onto the comfy brown couch that cornered one side of the living area, and laid her head back. The long flight had worn her out, and just as her eyes drifted close, the doorbell rang.

That must be my luggage, Ria thought. Her shoes sunk into the thick cream carpet as she jogged across the room and opened the door.

"Good evening, ma'am. Where would you like me to put these?" This time, it was a younger white male with an Italian accent.

"Hi. You can just put them here. Thanks." Ria took a five dollar bill and gave it to the young boy. She thanked him again before closing the high white door.

As she turned to face the beautiful apartment, Ria pinched herself to make sure she was not dreaming. She walked toward the huge window in the living room and pulled back the velvet curtains to stare at the view. The night sky and buildings stunned her. Though noisy outside, from inside of her apartment there was peace. Peace that she needed to move on. Ria drew the curtains closed. Already, she was starting to miss the blue sky and sunsets back home.

She stood there to reflect for a few moments before she remembered the pregnancy test in her bag. Should she throw it away? Did she really want to know if a love-child was taking bloom deep inside her? Ria walked toward where she had left her handbag and dug into it until she found the pregnancy test. She placed the kit on the coffee table, eyed it warily, and then took five steps away from it. She turned and glanced at it again. With the test hidden deep in her bag, she hadn't thought much about the possibility of being pregnant—out of sight, out of mind. But with the test resting on the table, it all suddenly seemed too real. She grabbed the test and marched off toward the bathroom. She removed the long plastic applicator from the box and stared at it while she twisted it in her hand. Right now, a baby did not fit into her plans.

Ria's hands shook as she followed the instructions on the box. With all the steps completed, the only thing she could do now was wait. She folded her hands beneath her breasts and paced while biting her lip.

Despite all the troubling thoughts tumbling in her head, she remembered a scripture in Psalms that her sister Chanel had told her: 'The Lord leads me beside still and peaceful waters.'

So blue is for positive, pink is negative. Ria said it again, reminding herself so that she would not get the two confused. She picked up the stick and held her breath. At the sight of the blue line, Ria gasped and held her stomach. Silence surrounded her. The sickness in the morning, the absence of her period, her emotions being out of sync, she could no longer deny the obvious.

Ria took a deep breath and exhaled slowly before going down to her knees on the bathroom floor. She cried until her heart felt like it was coming out of her chest. She had gone through one extreme emotion to another all in one day. She cried out Shawn's name three times, as if he could hear her. Sitting on the cold floor, she wrapped her arms around her knees. She never felt so alone and confused.

Chapter Seven

"What's this I'm hearing about you and Ria breaking up? I just can't believe it. Tell me that it's not that serious."

"I'm afraid that it is, Mrs. Sharon. I wish I could tell you different." Shawn sat talking with Ria's mother.

"I don't understand. After all you kids have been through—it's just not right! And I am not happy about this at all. I've only been gone a couple of years and it seems that things are falling apart all over the place. That daughter of mine does not know what she let go."

"Mrs. Sharon, don't blame Ria. You know I was the one who broke it off."

"Chanel told me everything, baby. But I'm sure if she stayed, you guys would still be together, right? I told her that a good man like you don't come around every day. And for her to leave you a year after your mother's death is just so cold hearted. I did not raise her to be like that. That girl is plain stiffed neck and stubborn just like her father." Sharon said with bitterness.

Shawn leaned back in a comfortable position.

"I can't blame her for going after her dream," he said. "There's no point in carrying on with something if you're going to have regrets." Shawn said.

"I thought you kids were going to get married and give me some grand-kids…I just don't know." Sharon said sighing.

There was not much Shawn could say to Ria's mother on the phone. Just like Sharon, he also once shared that same vision. Sharon and Shawn had a very close relationship. If you did not known any better, you would think that Shawn was Sharon's son. When Ria and Shawn were friends, Sharon always welcomed Shawn into her home. She treated him like the son she never had. She knew about his background and felt the need to take care of him. Shawn's natural mother was in and out of hospital with breast cancer throughout his college years. It seemed she had gotten better up until two year ago, when she was hit again with lung cancer which ended her life suddenly.

"You know what, Shawn, you have been like a son to me, and I will always be there for you. Never forget that."

"Thanks, Mrs. Sharon. That really means a lot."

Once the conversation ended, a wave of sadness came over him. It seemed that he was losing everything that was close to him. Shawn thought about his mother and how he and Ria used to drive up to the care home to visit her. He remembered Ria with a bunch of magazines in her hand, sitting there talking to his mother about who was hot and who was not. The tender care that Ria had showered on his mother during her last few months of life had made Shawn love her even more.

Shawn looked around at his apartment that suddenly felt cavernous and hollow without Ria's voice or presence. She had left behind nothing more than bittersweet memories and her familiar nutmeg-ginger scent. He grabbed one of the couch pillows, breathed in her fragrance from the fabric, and wept. Now more than ever, he longed for his mother's touch.

The Yandall Bar was a light-hearted bar run by an Irish couple. The place was small, but very popular. It had a nice atmosphere where people could come and chill and watch sports. There Kenny, Shawn and his friend Jonathan sat around a small round table.

"Well welcome to bachelorhood, man. Welcome to the club," Kenny said, patting Shawn on his back before sipping his bottle of beer. "You better thank God, bro, that she did not get pregnant. She would be nagging you for child support." Kenny said.

Kenny was older than Shawn by five years, but his bad living made him look much older. This was due to Kenny's alcoholic background and wild living, his caramel complexion showed evidence of premature wrinkles. One thing that Shawn and Kenny shared was their bright charismatic smile, which won the ladies every time. Even though they were a hit for the ladies, Kenny was bolder and knew how to wrap the ladies with his wit.

"Naw, man, Ria is good people. It's actually a shame that you guys don't have anything to show for it," Jonathan said, cutting into Kenny's annoying tone.

Jonathan was Shawn's friend from high school. They made friends after Jonathan got into a fight at high school and Shawn came to help him out. They both ended up getting their butts kicked and in detention. After that they hung out and after 20 years the friendship continued. Shawn was silent and sat with his broad shoulders hunched while resting his elbows on the small round table.

"Anyway, we did not come here to talk about the past," Kenny said, sounding annoyed. "We've come to congratulate my brother on being a football pro." Kenny patted Shawn's back again, which broke him out of his daze.

Shawn shyly smiled, then grinned, showing his pearly whites. "I can't believe it, man, I really can't. After all I've been through…I wish Mom was here to see it, though."

"I believe your mom knows, and she'd be really proud of you."

"Yeah, I believe so, too. Thanks."

As the night went on, Kenny became more and more intoxicated, which was one of the cycles that stopped him from progressing in his life.

Jonathan and Shawn continued the celebration even after Kenny had fallen into a drunken sleep in the corner.

"I better get him home," Shawn said as they both looked at Kenny and got up from the stools that surrounded the table.

A little more than a half-hour still proceeded till midnight when Shawn got back to his apartment. He dropped his drunken brother down on the couch, picked up a bucket from the kitchen, and put it beside him.

"You don't need that woman, bro. She was bad luck for you.

Seven years of bad luck!" Kenny said in a drunken slur. The phone rang as Shawn turned away from his brother. He picked up the handset.

"Hello Shawn." Ria's voice was soft, almost fragile.

"Hey Ria. Is everything all right? Did you reach New York safely?"

"Yeah, I kinda had a long flight, though. I was able to sleep a little. The apartment they put me up in is awesome."

An awkward silence stretched between them, and then they both tried to start a sentence at the same time. They both took small breaths of confidence.

"You go first," Ria said.

"Well, Ria, I did not get a chance to tell you that…I got picked up by the Stallions."

There was another breath of silence before Ria quickly responded, "I am so happy for you, Shawn. You, really do deserve it."

Ria was slightly relived that he had told her, but it still made her feel extremely uncomfortable to tell Shawn of her latest findings.

"So what was it you wanted to say?" Shawn said.

"Oh no, I just wanted to thank you for the money and the…ring it's beautiful, Shawn. It's the perfect fit."

It seemed as though they were strangers talking for the first time. Silence consumed the conversation again.

"Yeah, I meant to give you that a long time ago, but I never had the courage to give it to you." Shawn noticed a hint of distress in Ria's silence. "Are you all right, though, Ria?" In response to his question, Ria's eyes watered and her voice cracked.

"I'm okay. Just really tired."

"Are you sure?" Shawn always could read Ria's emotions well. He could always tell when she was hurting.

"I'll be all right," she said, whispering the last word.

"I better let you get some rest then. If you need me, just call me, okay?" Shawn said. *I need you now*, Ria wanted to say, but when she opened her mouth to speak, no sound came out.

"Have a goodnight, Ria."

"Goodbye, Shawn."

Shawn listened for Ria's line to hang up before replacing the phone on the base. She had said goodbye. Not goodnight. It was not like her to use those terms in a conversation with him.

Ria wanted to tell Shawn that he was going to be a father, but telling him would destroy his dreams. Things would just become too complicated and she knew that he hated drama. How could she tell the Editor-in-Chief that she was pregnant? And what would his response be in regards to her ability to perform as before? Ria felt a tight knot of emotions and indecision coiling in her stomach. Should she call Shawn back and tell him? Should she just get back on the plane and return home? Ria picked up the phone again and began to dial. She knew the exact person who would give reasoning and comfort in her distress.

"Hey Cissy."

"Is that you, Ri Ri?"

"Yeah."

"How is New York? You still don't sound too good. You still feeling sick?" Cissy asked.

"Everything is fine in New York, and I'm fine."

"You sound down."

"I've got some news to tell you. I think I'm pregnant."

Cissy gasp was so loud Ria heard it over the phone. "Oh my goodness, Ria, does Shawn know? Have you told him? What did he say?"

"I have not told him. I mean, I tried to, but I couldn't. I'm scared, Cissy. My mind is running all over the place."

"Well how many weeks are you?"

"I'm not sure. I took the home kit today, but I've yet to have it confirmed." Ria said. "Well wait until you see the doctor before you get all stressed out about it. Those home pregnancy tests aren't one hundred percent. You should really be going through this with Shawn though, Ri. He has a lot to do with what you're facing right now."

"Do you know he's been picked up by the Stallions?" Ria said.

"Really? I'm lost for words. How do you feel about that?" Cissy said.

"I'm confused, wondering whether I made the right choice. Cissy, he gave me a ring in an envelope."

"What kind of ring?"

"Engagement, he said he had it for a long time wanted to propose to me…but couldn't pluck up the courage."

"That's deep. Ri, you need to know that you made the right decision in yourself. I can't tell you that. It's never too late to come back."

As Ria listened to Cissy, she was reminded of the crap she encountered with Kenny.

"Anyway, I'm too tired right now. I'm gonna have to face this mess tomorrow." Ria said.

"Well, don't torment yourself tonight. Once you've rested, you'll have the strength to make a clear decision."

After talking to Cissy, Ria felt calmer and more relaxed. She pulled back the velvet comforter and slowly crawled into the bed while pushing the bed cushions aside. Her tired mind could think of nothing except sleep, hours' worth of fulfilling, uninterrupted sleep. She would contend with her battles in the morning.

Before closing her eyes, she stretched out her hand and grabbed one of the big silk cushions she had previously pushed aside, and held it close to her chest.

Chapter Eight

The wintery sun poked through Ria's dark curtains, causing her to stir out of her sleep. As she wiped her eyes, she felt much better. Her mind was clear, and there was an element of peace around her.

"I'd better get some breakfast before I head down to meet James," Ria said. As she wiped the sleep from her eyes, she got up and stepped onto her thick carpet, which reminded her of where she was. She took a look around her luxurious bedroom. It felt like a hotel and not a home. Everything was still alien to her. Before she entered the bathroom her phone rang.

"Welcome to New York, Miss Jackson," James said in a cool tone.

"Hi, James, how are you?"

"I'm downstairs, wanting to take you out for breakfast."

Ria half-wanted to believe the rumors about James and his swarm of women. She couldn't blame the women from sniffing around, what with James' physique and dreamy blue eyes. He worked out five times a week and had a physique of a man half his age.

"You're gonna have to give me like twenty minutes to get myself together. I just woke up. You can still come up though. I'll leave the door on the latch."

"Are you sure? I can come back if you need more time to beautify yourself for me." Ria laughed.

"You just get your butt up here," she said, smiling as she hung up.

After leaving the door on the latch, she rushed into the bathroom and turned on the shower. She groaned contently as the four showerheads gushed water over her skin. Ria marinated in the shower for nearly fifteen minutes before she stepped out of the rose-scented steam, grabbed a towel, and entered her cool bedroom. She inspected the room for her suitcases and forgot she had left them in the hallway. She tightened the blue towel and peeked around the door to see whether her suitcases were in sight. She looked up and down the hallway.

"James, is any of my suitcases in the living room?"

"Yes. Do you want me to bring them all over to you?"

"Oh no, just bring me, uh…the red one."

As James brought the suitcase to the door, he tried not to look at her in her towel and kept his attention on the suitcase. Ria noticed this and edged herself further behind the door.

She stuck her hand out. "I'll take it from here. Thanks, James."

"No problem."

Ria ironed her clothes, got dressed, and used hair grips to pin up her shoulder-length hair up. She walked out of her bedroom and into the living room. When James saw her, he rose from the couch and greeted Ria with a hug and a kiss on both her cheeks.

"We have a lot to talk about, James," Ria said with a sigh.

"Really now?" James said, lifting his thick black eyebrows and staring his blue eyes into Ria's oval-shaped ones.

Ria stepped back a little as she turned away from James to grab her bag and keys by the hallway. "I'm ready, let's go. We'll talk about it over breakfast. I am starving." Ria said.

"You like the apartment?" James asked as he followed after her.

"Oh my goodness, it is so beautiful, and stylish, and cozy."

"That's what I thought when I purchased it and—"

"It's your apartment? James, I knew you had a little taste, but this place is gorgeous!" Ria said interrupting James.

Though James had yet to confess it, Ria was aware James had a little soft spot for her. They just teased each other without overstepping the professional boundaries. As they walked out of

the lift, they easily blended into the hustle and bustle of Manhattan. The noise of cabs and cars and the pungent odor of exhaust fumes filled the air. It was quite a contrast to the quiet, peaceful apartment they had just come from. People were busily marching to their destination, hovering around and past each other like busy ants.

"Wow, it sure is fast over here," Ria said as she observed her surroundings.

"This is where it all happens!" James said, softly touching her lower back to direct her to a small restaurant down a side road. They entered the restaurant and the sweet aroma of fried eggs and bacon flavored the air. The restaurant was lightly decorated with wooden panels and framed pictures of famous Hollywood icons on the walls. The tables had little flower bunches with candles next to it, followed by the bench seats which were cushioned with a brown fake leather covering.

"Hmmm, it smells delicious in here," Ria said as they both located a table with vacant seats. They slid down on the bench seats and sat opposite each other.

Ria picked up the long, plastic-covered card and quickly scanned the menu for something reasonably priced and appetizing. "Hmmm, now let me see. I think I'll have a Spanish omelet with French toast, bacon, and two sausages. James, what are you getting?"

"I might just have the deluxe breakfast meal with a coffee."

Ria looked around to see if she could catch a waiter. She saw one who was only semi-occupied and signaled him over with her hand and a head nod. "Good morning, sir and madam. Are you ready to order?"

While James relayed both their orders, Ria observed him beneath the curtain of her long lashes. How would he react to her pregnancy?

As the waiter waddled off toward the kitchen, weaving in out of the many tables, James returned his attention to Ria.

"So, what's up? What's the latest news?"

"Well..." Ria said hesitantly. "Shawn and I broke off our

relationship."

"Really?" James said, nodding slowly while turning his amused expression into a serious one.

The waitress reappeared with a flask of coffee and a glass jug of orange juice balanced on a tray and placed it in the middle of the table.

"Yep, we are over. O-V-E-R." Ria took the jug of orange juice and poured it into the two glasses on the table.

"So, what happened then? Is it because of the job?"

"Partly, I think it's a combination of things. I mean..." Ria looked down at her glass of juice.

"I'm sorry to hear that, Ria. It must be tough, relocating and stuff. If you need some time to get yourself together, I can give you that."

"That's the least of my problems right now, James. I think I'm... pregnant."

James leaned back in his chair and stretched out his arm before partially covering his jaw line with his hand.

"Oh." He sounded a little disappointed.

"I did the pregnancy test yesterday, and it came up positive. I haven't told Shawn yet. I mean I tried to tell him yesterday, but I just couldn't. He just got signed with the Stallions, and it would change a lot of things, you know...it would be just too complicated."

"He does have the right to know if you're bringing his child into the world, Ria."

"I'll have to see what I'm going to do first before I tell him. I can understand if you have second thoughts on taking me on as the editor." Ria said in haste.

"Well, hold on a minute. I offered you the job on the basis of your skills and talents. I've known you for years and I know your work ethic and passion and I will still stand on that, whatever decision you make," James said, giving her a comforting smile.

"Thanks, James, I really appreciate that."

"So what are you doing for the holidays?" James said to lighten the atmosphere.

"I was planning to have a quiet Christmas for a change."

"Well you know you always have an open invitation to come and spend it with my family."

"Thank you, you are so good to me. I'll bear that in mind," she said with a flirtatious smile. The waitress appeared again with their hot steaming breakfast.

"Thanks," they said, one after the other.

"I can give you Dr Jackie Willberg's information," James said. "She's a good friend of mine, a doctor, and she has her own practice. She might be able to fit you in today as it goes. When you call her, tell her that you know me. It's worth getting that sorted out as soon as possible." James plunged a grilled tomato into his mouth and chewed hungrily. "Don't worry, Ria. Everything will be all right. If you need any support, I'm here for you and I will take care of you."

James rested his hand on her arm. "Are you still up to visiting the office, meeting the team?"

"Yep. I've got to keep moving. I came here to work, and that's what I'm gonna do."

"Okay. As long as you're all right. You don't officially start work until next week. So if you want to leave it for a couple of days, that would be fine."

"I don't need all that time, James. I just really want to get stuck in and find my rhythm."

They continued to talk about the structures and future plans of the magazine, and this helped Ria focus even more. She loved the print industry. It still had not fully hit her that she was now the editor of the magazine she loved.

As they finished their breakfast, they headed to the office. It felt so good to Ria to have someone comfort her and tell her she would be all right. It had been a long time since she'd had that support. Even though Ria's sister was a rock in her life, she still had not told her about being pregnant for fear that Chanel would tell her mother. And if Sharon was to find out, Ria could already feel the onslaught of accusation and disappointment that would drive her 'round the bend.

The cold breeze made Ria pull her jacket closer to her chest as she walked toward a tall gray building with revolving glass doors.

"You want my jacket? I almost forgot you're a California girl."

"No, Shawn—I mean James...I'm fine."

James looked at Ria and raised his eyebrows. As Ria used her hand to cover her slip, she felt awkward. Just when she was trying to move on, her soul was letting her down.

"I'm sorry about that, James."

"Don't worry about it."

As they walked through the door, Ria inhaled deeply. She was slightly taken back by the amount of people coming in and out of the revolving door. Everything looked polished and modern inside the building. The marble desk and leather seats by the door way made the building look extremely corporate.

"We're on the eighth floor. Really nice views," James said to Ria as he turned to her.

"It's so much busier here than the LA office."

"We only have one floor here, which is huge. It's nicely sectioned off into departments. Wait until you see your office."

As they moved in and out of the elevator onto the eighth floor, it seemed that the busy and pressured atmosphere had slowed down immensely. The atmosphere up here was much calmer and more tranquil.

"Welcome to Exhale magazine, New York. People are slightly different here than LA. Less gossip here, people just get on with their work. They are not necessarily friendlier—you'll see what I mean."

"Okay then," Ria said, slightly bewildered. She hated feeling like the new person at work.

After James had introduced Ria to the key team members, they headed to the back of the floor, which started to change in its presentation. Where the majority of the floor was an open plan, this side of the floor had huge offices, with massive dark oak doors decorated with numerous golden plaques. She glanced at the door that read: *Editor*.

"This is your office, Miss Jackson. I still have to clear some stuff out of the cabinets. That will be done by next week."

As Ria stepped inside the room, she was able to see a better view of the door, which also had her name stenciled beneath the editor title. The room was spacious and bright, and a huge mahogany desk positioned by the window took up nearly one-fourth of the room. She leaned over and looked out the window which took up two sides of the office wall, and admired the panoramic view. Was she dreaming or was this real? This was all slightly overwhelming—she had never had her own office before.

"It's such a beautiful view, especially at night," James said.

"I'm sure it is." Ria said.

"And that door there to your right leads to a small bathroom." James said.

His cell began to ring; he looked at it. "Do you mind if I step out for a minute? I really need to take this call."

"No, that's fine. It would give me a chance to see where I will put everything."

"Oh yes, before I forget, your office stuff from LA is under your desk. It was delivered yesterday."

"I'll get on with unpacking that then." Ria said.

"All right. I'm in the room opposite this one. Call me if you get stuck."

James exited the room and pulled the door close to grant her privacy. Like an excited child, Ria propped herself onto the large leather chair, and swiveled herself around with her leg extended out. She could not believe that all this was hers. It was unheard of to have an en suite bathroom in an office. As she continued to swing around on her chair, she suddenly stopped still, her happy thoughts snatched away and replaced with the tormenting thoughts of her pregnancy. Months from now her life could dramatically change. Maybe.

Chapter Nine

As soon as Ria returned to her apartment, she sat on the couch and turned on the television before she pulled off her shoes and messaged her pinky toe. She wondered whether she was getting the swollen pregnancy feet already.

Ria flicked through the channels and wondered what she would cook. It was strange cooking for one. She would normally cook what Shawn requested and ate what he ate. She never really took into consideration what she wanted to eat. Ria rested her hands on top of her abdomen and envisioned the tiny bean sprouting inside her. Her eyes drifted closed, and behind the privacy of her lids, she imagined what her life would be like with a baby. Or better yet, what would life be like as a single mother? She cringed at the thought.

She had promised herself that she would never be a part of the stereotypical statistic of being a single black mother—yet look at her. Somehow, she had managed to put herself in a boat very similar to Tandra. What if she ended up that way—three kids, three different baby daddies? This baby wasn't mandatory—there was always option B. But who was she kidding? Ria knew that she could not deal with killing her own child and then live with it on her conscience for the rest of her life.

Ria took the napkin that James had written Jackie's number on from the night stand. She leaned over to get the phone and dialed the number. It rang four times before an elderly sounding lady answered, "Hello, Dr. Willberg speaking."

"Hello, Dr. Willberg. My name is Ria Jackson. I'm a friend of

James Daniels. He gave me your number to call..." Ria hesitated.

"I would like to take a pregnancy test," Ria said.

"Okay, my dear, where are you located?"

"I'm in Manhattan," Ria said.

"Well, my clinic is also based in Manhattan. If you can get to me in an hour, I will squeeze you in before I head home."

"That will be very much appreciated, Dr. Willberg. Once I take the address I can jump in a taxi."

*****

Ria sat in the clinic, waiting for her results from the urine sample she had given to the nurse. She thought about Shawn and all that James had said to her. After finding out from Kenny what Shawn really thought about their relationship, Ria felt even less confident in telling Shawn. She did not want to trap him into a relationship just because she was carrying his child. And even more, Ria did not want to break her dream and go back to LA to face humiliation for not succeeding in anything she set out to achieve.

As she looked around the white and pale pink waiting room, she felt slightly humiliated sitting there, 'waiting for her results.' She had never imagined herself in this situation. In her mind, her husband was there, too, holding hands in anticipation. Deep down, she hoped that it was all a mistake. A baby was not what she had signed up for, and then to have to bring it up by herself seemed like a nightmare.

Fifteen minutes passed before Ria's name was called out by Dr. Willberg.

Ria got up from her seat and walked over to the gray-haired lady.

"Hello, Ms. Jackson. How are you?

"Hi, Dr. Willberg. I'm fine, just a little anxious."

Jackie Willberg's appearance looked just as Ria had imagined. She was a small-framed lady with long gray hair, small wrinkled features, but a kind face, and red lipstick that stained her two front

teeth.

"There's nothing to be worried about now. Bringing a new life into the world is very exciting."

Ria followed the woman into an unoccupied room, closed the door, and took a seat opposite Jackie.

Shaking like a leaf she spoke to herself quietly, *Pull it together, girl, pull it together,* but she could not help her heart from pounding.

"Well, your test results are very clear," Jackie said. "You're definitely pregnant. What we need to find out now is how pregnant you are. So tell me, when was the last time you had your menstrual cycle?" Ria hesitated. "I think my last period was about three months ago." Jackie looked at Ria surprised, which made Ria feel like an idiot.

"Have you missed a cycle before?"

"No, my periods have always been on time." Ria said. Jackie paused briefly and referred to a chart that she had in front of her.

"Okay, Ms. Jackson, you are probably about two to three months pregnant. That is just an estimate, as we are not too clear when you conceived. The only way we can get a more exact date is to give you a scan. Have you drank a lot of water today? We may need you to drink a couple of glasses so we can get a clearer picture."

Ria held her mouth with her hands to stop her from breaking down. Even though tears fell, exposing her true emotions, she remained in control.

"Dr. Willberg, this is all a bit much for me to take in. Two to three months pregnant? I'm not even showing. I'm not even sure if I'm going to keep the baby. I need some time to think about this."

Jackie frowned, making Ria feel worse for even thinking about terminating her pregnancy. Ria was also taken aback by the fact that she could be holding her own baby in her arms in only seven months.

"Ms. Jackson, to be honest with you, I have many young ladies coming into my clinic, wanting to terminate their pregnancies. I have seen the effect of what an abortion can do mentally. Please, have the scan done first. If you can see for yourself what you are giving up, then at least I have given you all the options."

"I'm not sure if I can handle a baby right now. I just started a job in a new state. There's a lot that I will have to sacrifice."

"Miss Jackson, some girls don't even have a job or a good friend that will pay for their medical care. You are in a very fortunate position, if you don't mind me saying." Jackie's comments made Ria reflect differently about her newfound situation. She never saw that she was more than capable of raising a baby by herself. Shawn had always been a part of any baby plans that she ever imagined. But now it did not seem like a nightmare. She knew that her new position would pay her enough money to give her and her baby a good lifestyle. *It might not be bad after all.* She thought.

"I'll have the scan done." Ria said.

Jackie picked up the phone on her desk and spoke to the nurse. She requested that she prepare the ultrasound equipment.

"Please, could you go out to the main hallway and turn to the first room on your right. The nurse will be there waiting for you. I will follow in a couple of minutes. Please, also try to drink about three cups of water? The water cooler is just in the waiting room."

Ria returned to the waiting room, drew a plastic cup from the water cooler, and filled it with water. Even though she felt better about the whole thing, she still was not completely convinced. Ria struggled with drinking the third cup of water. She took her time to swallow it. She wondered what Shawn's reaction would be. Would he be happy, sad, or impartial to the whole thing? As she swallowed the last few drops of water, her anxiety levels rose again.

Ria approached the room and eased herself on the bed. She greeted the nurse with a half-smile.

"Hi, ma'am," the nurse said. "Can you please lie on your back and lift your top so I can put this gel on your lower abdomen? It will be a bit cold, so I send my apologies in advance."

Jackie entered the room. "Thanks, I will continue from here. I know its past your time, so I will finish off with this patient and

see you tomorrow." Jackie smiled at the nurse as she left the room. Ria was lying on the bed, her belly exposed and covered with a thin layer of goo. Jackie switched the monitor on. Ria's heart raced as her uncontrolled breathing overtook her calm composure.

Jackie turned to Ria and noticed her chest heaving up and down. She took her hand and held it.

"Don't worry, I'm just going to put this part of the ultra-scan on your abdomen. What you will see on the screen won't be very recognizable, as you are still in the early stages of your pregnancy. But you will hear a heartbeat, and I will be able to do some measurements that will tell me how far along you are, all right?" Ria nodded and held Jackie's hand tight. It was at this moment that she wished Shawn was there with her. She needed him so much right now. As Jackie placed the ultra-scan on Ria's abdomen, she heard a beating echoing sound.

"Can you hear that, Ria? That's your baby's heartbeat. And here on the monitor is your baby's head..."

Ria was overwhelmed with what she saw. Was this moving creation living in her right now? It was hard for her to comprehend what was happening on the monitor as tears filled her eyes. The sound of her baby's heartbeat echoing throughout the room increased her anxiety of what she was going to do. Ria glued her eyes to the monitor; how could she kill something so precious, and innocent and made out of love. Whatever Ria decided she knew it would have to be a choice that she could live with for the rest of her life.

Chapter Ten

*I*t was strange not having Ria fussing around him on Christmas day. The smell of pumpkin pie flowing through the apartment was a smell he loved to hate, but now he missed it. There was not even a hint of tinsel to be found hanging on the wall. He normally left all of the decoration set-up for Ria because she loved doing it.

"It's just me and you then," Kenny stated as Shawn walked into the sitting room. He glanced at Kenny and the four cans of beers on the floor. He was glad that Jonathan had called to invite them both for Christmas dinner. He knew it would be difficult without Ria being there, but it was better than being alone with his drunken brother.

"Are you coming with me?" Shawn asked, aggravated.

"Yeah why not," Kenny said while attempting to get up from the couch. He fell back into the seat.

Shawn groaned. "You better sober up. Otherwise, I'm gonna leave your ass here, Kenny."

"And merry Christmas to you, too."

*****

Ria was curled up in her bed with a cup of hot chocolate with marshmallows. She had never spent Christmas by herself before. It came at the right time. It gave her time to think about the next stage of her life. Ria got up from her bed and sneaked a peek out of her apartment window and viewed the blanket of snow that covered Manhattan. She was so intrigued by the snow flakes and the beauty it possessed as it danced down from the sky. It was a complete contrast to what she was used to. Ria's mind could not help but think of Shawn; she wondered what he was doing for Christmas, whether he was cuddled up with his woman while she was alone and pregnant. After 10 minutes she crept back into her bed and snug back into the position she was in. Ria made an effort not to feel sorry for herself.

*****

Five months had passed since Ria had left Shawn for New York, and Shawn was enjoying the stardom he began to experience with the Stallions. He was a good athlete and played well on the field. His career was almost as hot as California's summer. It did not take long before he was a household name. Ever since he had moved with Kenny into his new house in Beverly Hills, he was living the dream that he always wanted. It was only in his still moments that he thought of Ria, on how it would have been good to share all of this with her. He missed her from time to time.

As Shawn entered the local shop in Beverly Hills, he approached the magazine stand and a copy of *Exhale* caught his eye. He smiled and just as he was going to pick it up, he was stopped by a small boy, no older than nine, with short blonde hair.

"Excuse me, sir. Are you Shawn Matthews?"

"Yes I am. How can I help you, little man?"

The little boy's eyes lit up.

"Oh, you are totally cool, sir. I'm your biggest fan. Can I have your autograph? When I grow up, I want to be just like you. I'm gonna play football."

"Wow, really. Make sure you get good grades in school and train hard, okay" Shawn said.

"Yes sir." The boy said as he ran over to his mother. "Mom, Mom! Do you have some paper and a pen?" The little boy said to his mom who was standing a few yards behind Shawn. Shawn turned around to see the excited boy's mother briskly walk up with

a shopping basket in her hand. "Hello, Mr. Matthews. My son admires you so much. He talks about you all the time." The mother said in excitement as she dug into her bag and grabbed a pen and note pad. The boy's mother gave the pen and the torn sheet of paper to Shawn.

He took the pen, smiled at her, and crouched down to the height of the little boy.

"What's your name, little man?"

"My name is David, sir."

"How about I get you some tickets to watch the Stallions play next season for you and your friends, if that's all right with your mom?"

The little boy slapped his dropped jaw with his little hands. He was speechless. As the little boy jumped around in excitement, his mother gave Shawn a hug. "You don't know how much this means to him. He really looks up to you."

"That's no problem. If you give me your contact information, I will pass it on to the office and they'll send the tickets out to you by the weekend."

"Oh, thank you, sir," the boy said. "I can't wait to tell my friends! They're not going to believe me."

As the excited mother and son walked off, Shawn returned his attention to the magazine stand. He picked up the issue of *Exhale* and skirted his eyes over the front cover. He looked attentively through the first few pages of advertisements, and then he stopped. There, before his eyes, was a picture of Ria. Shawn studied the headshot. Over the five months since she had been gone, her appearance had changed drastically. She had put on a couple of pounds, to say the least. The good memories of their relationship flooded his mind. It was a long time since they had spoken, and the last couple of times Shawn tried to contact Ria, he was left talking to her voicemail. He left it to the fact that she had moved on. He folded the magazine in half and placed it underneath his arm, picked up a box of orange juice, and proceeded to the checkout. As he made his way to his parked black Lexus, he saw a lady bending down into her car trunk. The lady wore a puzzled expression on her face as she popped in and out of her car trunk while holding her cell phone between her ear and shoulder. The woman was well-dressed with black, three-inch heels and a black, pin-striped skirt-suit. Her face was a beautiful tone of dark mahogany with captivating hazel eyes. She had a tall and slender frame, and her hair was neatly braided and tied in a bun.

As Shawn located his car, he pressed his car key remote control to unlock his car. "Excuse me, are you all right?" he asked while eyeing the lady's style from head to toe. As Shawn got closer, her face looked familiar.

The lady looked over at Shawn while catching her phone in her hand before it fell from between her shoulder and ear.

"I'm having a little car trouble. It's decided not to start, and I have a whole load of ice cream and frozen foods in the trunk." She held up one finger. "Excuse me for a minute." The lady returned her attention to her cell phone conversation.

"Hello, yes, so when are you able to send me out a replacement? Tomorrow! Can't you do anything sooner? Okay, okay, tomorrow at what time? I'll have to get a cab."

While the lady continued her conversation, Shawn sprinted to his car, opened it, and chucked the magazine and orange juice into the backseat. He then returned to the woman, and as he stared at her features, he remembered the lady's face from college. She was in the same business and finance class with him.

The lady flipped close her cell phone and took a deep breath. "I'm sorry about that. I have all this food in the trunk, which will not hold up in this heat. I'm gonna have to call a taxi. My garage dealer said they would collect it today, but my insurance company is going to send me out a replacement tomorrow."

"Where is your house located?"

"North Hollywood."

"Would you like me to drop you off?"

"Really, you don't need to do that. I'll catch a taxi. I wouldn't want to inconvenience you."

"It would not be a problem at all. By the way, did you use to go to..."

"Westwood College, business class, right?" she said finishing off Shawn's sentence. "I recognized you as soon as I saw you, but knowing who you are now, I didn't want to make a fuss. It's Shawn, right?"

"Yeah and you're, umm, Angela?"

"No. Andréa, Andréa La Salle." She said.

"Yes, Andréa, I was close. How are things? It's good to see you again." Shawn said feeling embarrassed.

"Apart from my car breaking down, I'm good, thanks..."

*****

After they had transferred the groceries into Shawn's car, they both got into opposite sides of the car. A blend of smooth jazz rhythms flowed from the stereo. Andréa settled herself in the car, buckled her seat belt, and allowed the music to ease her mind. She took a deep breath and exhaled softly.

"Hmm, smooth jazz? You don't look like the type of man that would appreciate this kind of music." Andrea said.

"I'm a smooth type of guy I have you know. I actually have a few jazz compilations here in the car."

Andréa chuckled. "A smooth type of guy? Well, that's a surprise to me because you seem like the type that listens to that awful rap music. I can't stand that stuff." Andrea said.

"Well I try to listen to all types of music, whatever fits the mood. To tell you the truth, I only started listening to jazz a year ago. Since then, I have learned to appreciate it. A sax is like a good vocal on a song. It's one instrument that carries so much emotion without words." Shawn said.

"Wow, I am impressed. I take my words back. Before I went to college, I wanted to be a jazz singer. Seeing my mother sing really inspired me. I guess that gift was passed on to me, but the reality of me singing in such a competitive industry was more than I thought I could handle at that time. So I decided to, well, drop it. I mean, I still sing sometimes..." Andréa said. She felt Shawn glance at her which made her feel shy. "So what have you done since you left college?" he asked.

"I went to Europe to study culinary skills. I spent about three years over there. I flew back and forth from LA to Europe until I met my ex, which brought me back to LA for good. I also missed home, too, so it was not just him that brought me back." A slight bitterness stemmed from Andréa's last comment, which Shawn picked up on. "Anyway, he was a record producer, so he would get me to cater food for his functions, and my gift opened doors for me, and here I am."

"You've done very well. I can remember you were always the very ambitious type. I admire that." Shawn was right, Andréa LaSalle, was her own boss and loved it. She provided catering services to only elite personalities.

"Well, I thank God that I had the faith to survive it. I've gone through so many storms. I'm not the naïve girl I used to be." Andrea said confidently.

"I see. By the way you're talking, I'm assuming you're a Christian, or is it born again? I'm not sure what phrase to use now."

"You're not doing too bad. I would qualify as a born again Christian."

"What led you to become a Christian?"

"A broken heart." Andrea said.

"I've had one of those, and I'm still healing," Shawn said with a smile.

"What? You, a broken heart? Oh, come on. You must have women falling at your feet all the time. I remember on campus, all the girls were chasing you."

"That's real love is it?" He said.

"I suppose you're right. Especially in the sports industry, it's hard to find love, or even worst, most of y'all turning gay or on the down low," Andréa said, emphasizing a Southern accent with a touch of bitterness again. The only real relationship Andréa had was a ten-year engagement, which ended with her fiancé announcing that he was gay and needed to come out of the closet and be free. Since ending that relationship three years ago, Andréa had tried to focus on her career and establish herself. Her girlfriends encouraged her to not give up on the love game, but what they could not understand was that she was still hurting and broken inside.

"Ouch. Sounds like *A Diary of an Angry Black Woman* Part Two."

"Well, when a woman's fed up, there ain't nothing you can do about it."

"Well, let me represent for the few good, *straight*, black guys out here," Shawn said, tapping his broad chest with his left hand, while holding the wheel with his right. They both laughed. "So you can sing, huh? Hmm, interesting...sing me a line?" Shawn said, changing the subject.

"Oh, no way. I am not singing in your car. I've got to be in the right mood. Real singing is an art and a gift and..."

"Tut, tut, all of these excuses"

"All right. All right, Shawn, I'll sing to you when we get to my apartment. What do you want me to sing?"

"Something special, just for me. Something to heal a broken heart." Shawn smiled.

"Let me think on it, and I'll see what I can rustle up." She stared out the window, watching a few cars pass by, then turned to Shawn and said, "Do you remember Mr. Kass? He got replaced by Mr. Johnson. That man used to always come in drunk. Do you remember him?" Andrea said.

"Yeah, I do. Didn't he used to nominate a member of the class to teach a topic, and if you messed up, he would give the whole class a test?" Shawn said while he chuckled. "Shawn, I remember when it was your turn to teach. I was quite impressed on the way you conducted yourself and the class. You were teaching on risk management." Andrea said coyly.

"My goodness, you do have a good memory. I remember doing some kind of presentation back then, but to what it was, I have no idea. A lot was going on back then."

Shawn and Andréa continued to reminisce on their college years as the sun began to set behind the clouds. Following

Andréa's directions, Shawn pulled into her housing complex, stepped out the car, and assisted her with her grocery bags.

As they both came out of the elevator and walked toward Andréa's door, she opened it and rested her back against the door for Shawn to pass with the groceries. When Shawn passed by Andréa, his cologne snaked through her nose, making her groan silently to herself as she inhaled it. She thought those college years of crushing on Shawn Matthews were over. He didn't even know it, but he had managed to crush her heart when that a girl from his English lit class caught his eye and he started dating her. After college, Shawn and Andréa hadn't kept in touch, and her quiet crush on him had slowly extinguished itself over the years.

"Thank you so much, Shawn, for helping me."

"It was so nice seeing you again, Angela—I mean Andréa." Andrea rolled her eyes. "Is Angela one of your girlfriends, or is it the one you were chasing in your English lit class?"

"Chasing? I don't quite remember that."

Shawn smiled, knowing what Andréa was teasing him about.

"Once Miss thang came on the scene, you dropped me like hot baked bread."

"I really don't remember that. Did we date?" Shawn asked with curiosity, while still maintaining his cheeky smile.

"No, we were just good friends. I'm just teasing you?" Andrea said.

"I had so much on my mind back then."

"I see, how to manage all those girls must have taken up a lot of brain activity." Andrea said.

"Why are you trying to make out like I was a player? I only dated one girl in college."

"I'm playing, Shawn." Andréa grinned, lightly placing her hand on his muscled arm. "Do you want to stay for something to eat, a little light lunch?"

"It depends on what's on the menu," Shawn said.

"I was thinking a little steamed haddock, creamy potatoes in parsley and mustard sauce, with a side dish of buttered mushrooms and onions. Does that interest you?"

"It does indeed. You know the saying, a way to a man's heart is through his stomach."

"We'll just have to see if I'm successful or not. I like a challenge." She said.

Andréa took a closer look at Shawn, she wondered if he was single. She didn't notice a wedding band on his finger as she was talking to him.

"Please make yourself at home, Shawn. Have a seat." Shawn pulled up a stool from beneath the pinewood breakfast table.

"It's been a long time since I had a good home-cooked meal."

"Really? Don't you have…" Andréa wanted to just come out and ask whether he had a girlfriend or not, but she didn't want to seem too forward. "a cook? Most of you guys have personal chefs that help with your diet. If they don't have any wives or girlfriends, that is."

"Well, I can cook myself, but I'm on the road a lot, so I don't get the opportunity to go for those services. I'm a private person, too, so I don't like too many people coming in and out of my home." Shawn knew what Andréa was fishing for. He smiled. "I'm a bachelor, so you know how it is."

Andréa turned to the refrigerator to get the haddock out. She grinned without Shawn seeing her. One thing that still remained with her even after all these years was that Shawn was still a gentleman. "So, Andréa, what about that song you were going to sing to me? Have you thought of something? Anything by Anita Baker will do."

Andréa put down the parsley and walked over to Shawn and stood in front of him. As Andréa started to sing, she focused her hazel eyes on his darker ones, and captivated him with each note and expression.

"*When I'm calling out your name, I feel no shame,*" she sang. Shawn was indeed mesmerized by her vocal ability and sensuality. He smiled as he remembered how Ria used to serenade him. After Andréa finished singing the chorus, Shawn applauded her.

"That was nice. You've got quite a talent there. Yes, I'm impressed, really impressed. So they teach you that type of stuff in

church, then?" Shawn teased.

"No, I learnt that one all by myself," she said with a pleased smile, suddenly feeling shy. She knew that she had impressed him. She returned her attention to the parsley leaves and brought out her glass chopping board.

"So did that mend your broken heart?" she asked.

"I think I will need some extra doses of it, maybe three times a day." Shawn said.

"Well, we will have to see about that."

Chapter Eleven

"Sonia, you'll never guess who I saw earlier today!" Andrea said excitedly.

"Who?"

"Take your mind back to our college years."

Sonia was Andréa's best friend from college. She was one of her devoted friends who helped her through her traumatic break-up.

"Who…Tammy?"

"No, guess again."

"Andréa, just tell me. I'm never going to get it."

"Shawn Matthews." Andrea said eagerly.

"Oh, I see. Ain't he playing football now or something?" Sonia said. "Yes he is, and he is very single." Andréa was so excited, but it seemed that Sonia was not as thrilled as she was.

"So where did you see him? Did he even remember you?" Sonia said.

"Of course he did. It all happened when my car broke down, and he came to my rescue."

"Is he a Christian?"

"I don't know that yet. We did not have time to discuss that while he was at my house." Sonia walked over to her office door and closed it before taking her phone off the loud speaker.

"He came to your house? Look, you better be careful. Those football pros are dangerous as hell." Sonia said sternly.

"He's different. He actually said that his heart had been broken." Andrea said defensively. "Broken by what, may I ask?"

Sonia was not impressed at all. She could tell that Andréa was overexcited, which concerned her greatly.

"Why you got to be so negative about it? I just spoke to the guy."

"I'm not being negative, honey, just realistic. Do you remember how much pain you went through with that gay fiancé of yours?"

"Now why did you have to go there?"

"I just don't want to see you hurting again. I suppose you exchanged numbers?" Sonia said.

"Yes," Andréa said confidently.

"Hmm, I would not trust his type at all." Andréa rolled her eyes. Why did Sonia have to rain on her parade? Andréa decided to change the topic. "How's your day been?"

"From the sounds of it, not as good as yours. My day is going fine. I hope you're coming to Bible study tonight. Do you want me to pick you up?"

"I don't know. I've got a few things to do." Andrea said. So what if she was lying? Andréa did not feel like spending her evening with Sonia when she was in her little mood—especially since Andréa did not have her own car. It meant that she would be at the mercy of Sonia until she got home. Sonia was the type to spend far too long in church after service had finished.

"Like what, daydream about Shawn Matthews all evening? I know you to well Andrea. I'll pick you up at seven." Sonia said sternly.

As much as Andréa loved Sonia, she hated when she acted as though she knew everything. *How does she know I will be daydreaming about Shawn all evening?* Andréa thought.

As Andréa prepared her Caribbean fruit salad, her cell phone vibrated from the pocket of her apron. She looked at the face of the cell and saw that she had received a text message. Her face lit up as if someone had just told her she had won a million dollars. It read:

It was nice seeing u today, u have become such a beautiful woman. Hope 2 c u again. Shawn M.

If anything bad happened that day, it wouldn't matter to Andréa. She was walking on the moon. It had been such a long time since Andréa had received a compliment from a man, and then to get one from someone she still adored seemed too good to be true. Whatever Sonia was ready to bring tonight at Bible study, she was ready for it. She was now in her own romantic island called daydream.

*****

Ria sat on her couch with one foot propped up on the coffee table and one hand resting atop her protruding round belly.

"Miss J, should I email over page five to publications?" Ria's personal assistant asked as she walked over with a glass of ice cold water.

Ria took the water from her and swallowed a refreshing gulp. "Yeah, email page five and two, those are the ones I reviewed. Thanks, sweetie."

"Is there anything else you need, Miss J?"

"No, baby, I'll be okay. It's Friday anyway, so go home early." Ria reached for her stereo remote control and turned on the CD player, then flipped through the tracks of Will Downing's CD until she found her favorite song. She loved his music.

Ria's cell phone rang, and she pressed pause on the CD player. She looked at her cell, but could not recognize the caller. Curiously, she answered the call.

"Hello" Ria said.

"Hello, Ria. Is that you? It's Shawn." It felt like Ria's heart stopped for about a minute before she could respond.

"Shawn, how are you? It's been some time since we last spoke."

"Yeah, I know. I'm in New York for a couple of days, wondered whether you wanted to meet up."

"Well..." Ria looked down at her belly again. Should she tell him? "Shawn, I would love to, but I've had the flu for the past few weeks and my strength still has not picked up yet." Shawn was disappointed. "No worries, we'll catch each other some other time. I bumped into James last night, and he said that I should really try to see you..." Shawn added.

"Really, now?" Ria rolled her eyes to the ceiling. "How is football?"

"It's cool, you know. I'm trying to do my best out there."

"I'm happy for you." Ria said.

"I'm missing you though, Ria. And I just wanted to…"

Ria's house phone rang, interrupting whatever else Shawn was about to say. She could tell from Shawn's tone that the love he felt for her was still there.

"Shawn, I have to let you go. My house phone is ringing. I'll call you back in ten."

"Okay, but..." Shawn was unable to finish his sentence. Ria ended the call and dropped her cell on the couch. She waddled over to pick up her house phone.

"Hello?"

"Ria, it's your mother."

"Oh!" Ria said sarcastically.

"What do you mean, oh? Anyway, Ria, what is going on with you keeping secrets from the family?"

"Mom, what are you talking about?"

"Well, you're about to be a mother in a month's time. What do you think I am talking about?"

"Mom, I was going to tell you when I was good and ready."

"When would that be? When the child is celebrating its first birthday? I don't understand why you always keeping stuff from me, Ria."

"Look, Mom, I really don't want to argue with you about this right now."

"Have you told Shawn yet? That's a good man you let go. Look at the mess you've gotten yourself into."

"Mom, you have no idea what the situation is, and I would appreciate it if you mind your own business," Ria said sternly.

"Excuse me, child? You better remember—"

"No, Mom, you better remember that I am a grown woman, so

keep your nose and your business in Barbados." Ria hung up the receiver. She knew that Chanel was the one who had told her mother about the pregnancy. Ria hated disrespecting her mom in that manner. Every time they spoke, it always seemed to turn into an argument.

Having her mother a few thousand miles away in Barbados suited Ria quite well. It meant that she could get on with her life without the constant interference of her mother in her business.

Ria returned to the couch, still irritated by the argument. But as her anger waned away, she began to see the truth of her mother's comments. The only regret Ria had now was not telling Shawn sooner. With each day that passed, it grew more and more difficult to tell Shawn, especially now that he was in the public eye. She could not face speaking to him after the conversation with her mother. Would he hate her for not telling him sooner? Could he understand her reasoning for keeping this pregnancy to herself? Or would he accept the baby in his life, but shut her out for her betrayal?

As Ria pushed these thoughts and her weariness to the back of her mind, she reflected on her life and wondered on the things she would do differently if she had a chance to do it all over again. Even though she was in a new season, Ria wanted a fresh change, a complete change. It seemed that she still had a noose around her neck, and she wanted to be free. Since the pregnancy, she found it difficult not having the strength to get up and do the things she wanted to do. Ria wanted her life back to the norm with no baggage, no babies, and no dilemmas, just a bright independent future.

She looked down at her milk-filled breast and swollen feet, and she laughed at herself. She was at the stage of either crying or laughing about the situation. James would often attend hospital appointments with her, which helped her emotionally since her hormones were working overtime. The flip-side to this was that it brought a lot of speculation in the office to whether Ria was carrying James' baby. Ria did not concern herself with the gossip floating around about her. In her eyes, she had bigger fish to fry.

Chapter Twelve

$\mathcal{G}$t was about four o'clock when James left Ria's apartment after dropping her home from the office. Ria waddled over to the huge white windows and opened them wide. As the breeze entered through the window and flowed into the stuffy living room, she exhaled. Ria was exhausted from the sleepless night she had the night before. Even though James had offered to stay around until the morning, Ria had kindly declined his offer. She was grateful for his support, but she did not want to send any wrong signals. After all, he was still her boss.

Ria turned on the TV and opened a container of Chinese food that she had picked up with James. She sat on her couch and ate her orange chicken and steamed rice, she flicked through the channels. She stopped at a wildlife documentary, and as she watched the lonesome tiger, prowling the dry, deserted land, she realized the extent of her loneliness. She was fed up with going through the same routine each and every day. Glancing around at the hollowness of her apartment, Ria momentarily contemplated moving back to LA. As beautiful as her apartment was, she realized how much she missed her friends, her sister, and all that was familiar to her.

After Ria had eaten half her food, she placed the container on the table top. She returned to the couch and dozed off for an hour before suddenly awakening to a sharp pain in her abdomen. She groaned as the sharp pain hit her again. Ria lay still, waiting for the pain to cease. As it passed, she took a deep breath and tried to stand. All of a sudden, the pain hit her again. This time, the pain shot through her whole back. Ria stooped to her knees with her elbows supporting her. She put her head between her elbows and cried out. She located her cell phone, which was an arm's length away, and clutched the phone tightly in her shaky hand. Should she call the emergency services? Since she still had a month to go before her due date, wouldn't this be considered premature labor?

Drenched in fear and confusion, she decided to call Shawn. She really needed him—she was scared. As the pain eased, she collected her senses, but kept herself in the crouching position. Desperate, her fingers trembling, Ria searched through her phone book for Shawn's number. Thinking quick she located his LA cell number and called it, she knew he would be back home by now. She dialed the number, and held her breath as she listened to the phone ring.

"Hello, Shawn's phone."

"Who's this?" Ria asked, surprised that a woman had answered Shawn's phone.

"This is Andréa. Who is it you want to speak to please?"

"Shawn, I need to speak to Shawn."

"Okay, could you hold the line?" Her voice moved away from the speaker. "How do I put this phone on hold? Shawn! There's a lady on the phone for you."

"Who is it, honey?"

"I didn't get her name."

"Can you take a message? I'm just about to step in the shower!"

Ria could hear the communication between the two of them on her side of the phone. Andréa returned to the phone, a little irritated.

"He's busy," she said.

"Tell him it's Ria, and he needs to call me ASAP."

"Ria who?"

"He knows who I am." Ria ended the call.

As she began to slowly lift herself up from the position she was in, the pain hit her again. Ria dropped down to her knees. At that moment Ria felt a gush flow down her thighs. She needed help quick. As the pain eased away once again, Ria got up from her kneeling position, but felt dizzy. She reached for her house phone and called Derek, the clerk at the reception desk.

"Derek, I think my water's broken. I need an ambulance right now." Ria slurred her last word and collapsed on the floor.

*****

As Andréa sat exhausted on her couch, Sonia sat beside her with her legs crossed. "So what's going on?" Sonia asked. "You don't pick up my calls, I haven't seen you in church for the longest time."

"Sonia, I have been busy," Andréa said while flicking through a magazine.

"So after 12 years of friendship, you're too busy to pick up my calls?"

"I'm really not in the mood for one of your lectures." Andrea said.

Sonia looked at Andréa with a stare that penetrated right through Andréa. "I did not come here to lecture you," Sonia said. "I came here because I am concerned about you—we all are. Janet and I were talking and…"

"You and Janet were discussing my business behind my back? How dare you," Andréa said with venom.

Sonia got up from her seat, shocked. "What is your problem? Just because one man finds interest in you, you lose interest in everyone that cares about you. You've had a strong soul tie for this man for too long, and it's not healthy. I pray to God that it is broken before it does more harm than it has already."

"Whatever, Sonia. The only soul tie that I can really see is the one from you to me. You want me to stay single like you for the rest of my life? Hell no. Don't let the door hit you on your way out."

Sonia was astounded. She picked up her bag with hurt in her heart and saw herself out.

Andréa could not stop herself from loving Shawn. She knew

there was truth in what Sonia was saying. But for some reason, this made her even more determined to prove her friends wrong. There was no way Andréa was going to return back to her single life. Having a man around eased the pressure and emotional weakness she had suffered as a single woman.

"It will work, I know it will. God, please make this work", Andréa said while she looked up at her ceiling. Andréa felt bad; she knew Sonia was speaking out of love.

Andréa quickly ran out to try to catch Sonia. She managed to catch her as Sonia started the ignition.

"Sonia, Sonia! Girl, look I'm sorry, I had no right talking to you like that."

Sonia looked at Andréa with a slight frown which highlighted her thick eyes brows and long black eyelashes. "I would have expected that crap from anyone else but you."

"I know and I'm truly sorry," Andréa said slightly ashamed. She opened Sonia's car door and sat. "It's been crazy and I feel like I'm at a crossroads. On one hand I'm in love with a man that treats me like a queen. Yes we seem to be living in so called *sin*, but he makes me happy. If I stop this, then what do I go home to? I can't go back to that single life again."

Sonia listened as Andréa poured out her heart. "There's just something about your relationship that concerns me, Andréa. I hear you. I've been single for eight years. But I'm still holding onto my faith that God will supply my every need. I will not settle for being second best."

Andréa placed her hand on Sonia. "You've got the faith for that, and I don't. Maybe God will save Shawn. He has been to church."

Sonia hesitated and held Andréa's slim fingers in her chubby hand. "That's what they all say, baby. You just come back to church, okay? Even if it's just on Sundays. You can hide from church, but you can't hide from God." Sonia said.

After they said their goodbyes, Andréa went into her home and attempted to get herself ready as Shawn was on his way to pick her up for a dinner date. Andréa had suggested this to Shawn as there was a growing distance starting to form between them. She thought at the time that it would give them time to talk in a different atmosphere which could not end in the bedroom.

When Shawn arrived, she greeted him with a kiss and was reminded of the distance. They had shared no more than five words since Andréa slid into his car.

As they neared the restaurant, she knew she could not spend another moment with Shawn unless they talked. She turned to face him and stared at his strong, hard jaw line—and the tight way he held the steering wheel.

"So what's the matter?" she asked.

"What do you mean?"

"Shawn, you have been moody with me for the better part of the week. And I am starting to get fed up with it. You're giving one-word answers when I'm trying to talk to you. Shawn remained silent, which made Andréa even more frustrated. Andréa took in a deep breath. "Look, Shawn, can you just drop me off at home?"

"But I have made reservations!" He said.

"I just want to go home right now."

"No problem," Shawn said sharply. He was relieved that Andréa had decided to go home. It seemed lately that he was going through emotions that he could not understand, and he needed time to think. He was falling for Andréa. He connected with her sweet spirit, but lately, he often felt sick to his stomach every time he spent time with her.

"I think we need some space, Andréa," he finally said. "There's a lot going on in me right now. It's not you, it's me."

"Don't give me that line, Shawn. If you want to end this relationship, then be a man and just say it. I have tried to be there for you, I really have. If it's not working for you, just tell me straight."

Andréa looked at Shawn and waited for a response as they stopped outside of her apartment complex. As he turned to face her, she looked into his eyes, searching for an emotion of some kind.

"Andréa, please don't be mad at me." Shawn took her hand

and caressed it with his thumb. "Honey, look, I wish I could explain what I'm going through right now, but I don't know myself. I just need time to get my self together. I don't want to mess up this time, and I don't want to lose you." His words managed to calm Andréa from her brash statement. She saw the sincerity in Shawn's eyes and felt comforted.

"Okay, Shawn. I'll wait for you, but I can't wait forever."

"I'm not asking for you to wait forever. I just need some time." Shawn kissed Andréa's hand and watched with saddened eyes as she exited the car.

Chapter Thirteen

As Ria opened her eyes, she could hear someone calling her name, a voice that she did not recognize.

She allowed her eyes to adjust and focus on her surroundings, and she felt a prick on the front of her wrist. Ria looked down, and from her blurred vision, she saw an IV stuck in her wrist.

"Miss Jackson…"

Ria tried to let out a word, but it came out muffled from the oxygen mask surrounding her mouth. Ria felt a warm touch on her hand.

"Shawn? Shawn, is that you?" In an elevated position, Ria looked to her left.

"Ria, it's James. Everything is going to be all right."

Ria looked into his blue eyes as if she was a scared kitten. She gripped his hand tightly. Then, she felt all of her senses slowly returning as she looked down at her round belly with a belt around it and observed a lady who looked troubled by what she was seeing on the monitor.

Ria loosened her grip from James' hand and lowered her oxygen mask from her face.

"What's going on? What's wrong with my baby?"

Ria began to panic, her heart pounding like an African drum.

"Miss Jackson, I'm Dr. Kimber. We need you to stay calm, okay? You and your baby are in good hands."

A stern masculine voice came from behind her. "Miss Jackson, we have to perform an emergency caesarean since your baby is in distress and his heart rate is starting to fall."

Ria felt powerless and weak. She could feel some pressure on her back, but still felt disoriented in her unfamiliar surroundings.

"We're going to prep you for surgery," the man said. "We're going to give you a general anesthetic. Please, could you read and sign these documents?"

Bewildered, she looked over at James. Ria took the documents on a clipboard with a pen attached to it. She took a deep breath, collected her emotions, and tried to think straight. She read what she could and signed where needed.

After she had completed the forms, the man removed the belt from around her protruding belly. An elderly woman with a pleasant face approached her bedside.

"Hello, Miss Jackson, my name is Helen. I will be here to support you. Can you change into this operating dress? I will be with you throughout this whole process." Helen drew closer and whispered, "Don't worry. God is with you."

Her last words echoed in Ria's heart, and a wave of calm came over her. From there, everything else became like watching a movie, and her responses went into auto-pilot mode. She did not feel worried, anxious, or troubled.

"Ria, I will be waiting outside." James said flustered.

Though she saw his lips move, Ria had no idea what James had said to her. Her auto-pilot mode was operating at full force.

Everyone left her room except for Helen the nurse, who closed the door and assisted Ria with undressing and putting her hospital dress on. Helen's aura of calm filled the room.

"There you go. You really have nothing to worry about. Everything is going to be okay, sweet lady."

Ria nodded as she eased back onto the bed and settled into a more comfortable position. "I'll be back in just a minute. The doctors will be coming in very soon."

"I'll be in the room with you when it all happens," James said, peeking his head through the door.

"Your partner is very sweet. You have a good man out there."

As Helen exited the room, the stern doctor entered with

another doctor and a nurse.

"Okay, Miss Jackson, we are going to take you down to the delivery theatre…"

The doctor continued to speak to her, but it seemed as though her hearing had went out, and she was participating in a Charlie Chaplin silent movie. As the bed rolled out of the room, Ria looked up at the ceiling and counted the lights passing her by. While she mentally counted each one, her eyes began to feel heavy and she closed them.

*****

In what felt like a split-second, Ria opened her eyes and found herself back in the room she had just left. When she tried to move up from her bed, she felt tightness in her lower abdomen. She looked down and her once protruding belly had reduced to half its size. Just before she could panic, she heard a female voice.

"Congratulations Mommy! I have a gift for you to see, that's if you're ready for it."

Helen helped prop Ria in a comfortable sitting position. Before Ria knew it, Helen had placed a small moving bundle in her arms. Ria took her baby in anticipation, and as she stared into his tiny face, she could not quite believe that she was holding her child in her arms. She felt strange and could not quite grasp the concept of her being a mother. It had all happened so quickly, she could not remember having to push and scream like Chanel had. It all felt surreal. She quickly scanned the baby's small fingers and toes, counting five of each. "Are you sure he's mine? I can't quite believe that I am holding my baby in my arms."

"I guarantee that he's yours, my dear."

"Is it okay? Does it have anything wrong? I was not expecting until next month."

"*He* is perfect. Sometimes it's a give and take with the estimated time of conception and delivery date. He's had all the checks and the doctors are happy with him. Boy, did he let out a roar when he came out."

"He's…a boy. My son…" She stared down at him, shaking her head in amazement. "I'm just so caught up in just holding my baby. It just seemed to happen so fast," Ria said, smiling and still drowsy from the anesthetic.

She looked into his face and studied him silently. His little brown eyes searched her face, trying to focus. As her baby yawned, she saw Shawn in him.

"You look just like your daddy when you do that."

Staring into her son's eyes, all the anxiety and frustration she had felt had vanished. She wanted Shawn with her. As she continued gazing at her son, she thought about what Shawn would have said and done at the thought of holding his own son.

Helen interrupted gently. "I think he might be a little hungry. Breastfeeding also helps the bonding process, especially since you had a caesarean."

"You mean I got to breast feed him now?"

"Yes, all you need to do is put the whole nipple into his mouth, even the outer darker part, and he will do the rest."

"Won't he choke with all that in his mouth?"

Ria had seen her sister breastfeed her child, but it never really came to her realization on how to do the whole thing. As Ria pulled down her gown, she found herself naturally feeding her baby.

"You must have some strong negro genes, ma'am. He don't look nothing like his daddy."

Ria looked at Helen, and for the first time, assessed her face. Not wanting to spoil the mood, Ria dismissed Helen's comments and voluntarily turned her attention back to her son. As her baby drifted off to sleep, Ria removed her nipple from his mouth and covered herself back up.

"He's outside waiting for you. Should I call him in? He's been pacing up and down the hallway—I'm surprised he's not made a hole in the floor." Helen remarked.

"Oh, I almost forgot…I think I'm okay to receive vis…" Ria stopped herself before she completed her sentence. Helen looked at her questionably, already knowing the end of the sentence.

"Okay…I'll send your vis-it-or in."

James popped his head through the door before fully entering.

"Oh, James, come and have a look at him. He's beautiful." James hastened over to her bedside. "You have done very well, Ria. I'm so proud of you. He is a cute little one. Look at his little face. I almost had a heart attack when Derek called me." James smiled, revealing his dimples.

"James, thank you. I couldn't have done this without you. You have been there for me all the way."

James took a seat in the chair beside Ria's bed. "I've been thinking for a little while to relocate you back to LA."

"What!" Ria's surprise was evident on her face.

"It's gonna be almost impossible for you to raise a child out here in this city. You have no family here to support you. It's gonna be hard for you, Ria. At least back in LA, you'll have your family, your sister, friends." James scooted to the edge of his chair and looked into Ria's eyes. "If things were different, I would invite you to share my life. I would look after you and your son. But I know that you are still deeply in love with Shawn. And now that you have his child…well, I wouldn't want to get in the way of that."

Ria knew that James was right. Whether she liked it or not, she still had not gotten over Shawn. Something that should have been a temporary break between them had turned into a break-up. Now, she was holding his child—an equal part of him—in her arms. She had only spent five months in New York, and now, she would be coming back home to face the music.

"You can see that much in me, James?"

"You are not the same Ria I used to know. You really need to get back home and sort things out."

"What am I going to do, huh?" Ria said shaking her head in slight distress.

"Don't get yourself stressed about it. Take your time. I'll set you up with a home office once you settle back in LA. Anyway, we'll talk about that later. Concentrate on recovering, okay?" James kissed Ria on the forehead before he left her alone, holding her sleeping baby. After James left, she wondered about life back in LA. She thought about being with James. She loved him, but it was not in that way. Since Ria had moved to New York, James had treated her like a queen; she lacked nothing. What an indeed mess she had gotten herself into. Even though Ria was holding her baby, she still felt like she had ended up with the short stick.

Chapter Fourteen

*K*enny let out a shriek of laughter as he snorted the powdered substance from Shawn's glass coffee table. "That is the good stuff, man. Where'd you get it?"

"Special connections," Kenny's friend, Max mumbled while snorting from the opposite side of the table.

"Look, my brother gonna be back here later. I've got to get this place cleaned up." Kenny stood, shook his head, and wiped his nostrils before he gained his senses.

"It was a good party, man. Look at that chick on the floor. She out of it," Max said giggling.

"Yeah, she better be out of here right about now."

Kenny walked over to the Puerto Rican woman sprawled on her stomach on the floor, her silver short lycra dress hiked up on one side.

"Hey, Tatiana get up, party over," Kenny said while tapping her with his foot. She stirred from her embarrassing state and staggered to her feet. In dismay, she looked around her surroundings, searching for her friend. She gazed across the blue carpet and spotted her friend on the huge leather couch.

"Hey, Miss, the door is that a way."

"I'm going to get my friend. Is that all right with you?" Tatiana looked Kenny dead in the eye before she cut her eyes and continued on toward her friend. "Hey, get up. We got to go."

The lady on the couch jumped up as if she was resuscitated from the dead. "Tatiana, I don't feel so good. I feel like I'm gonna be…"

Tatiana's friend bent over and allowed the contents of her stomach to decorate the floor. Tatiana held back her friend's hair while she continued her artwork of vomit on the floor.

"What the…"

Kenny rushed over to them and grabbed them both by their skinny limbs. Drips of vomit still protruded from the girl's mouth.

"Look, you stupid chicken-heads, get the hell out of my house."

As Kenny chucked the two ladies out the front door, one of them continued to vomit outside. He returned back to the destruction of the house that he had less than three hours to clean. Bottles and beer cans were all over the place, along with people littered throughout the house.

"Hey, hey everybody! Party over, you got to go. You got to get the hell out of my house right now."

Kenny went throughout the living room area, clapping his hands and shouting at the top of his lungs like a dictator commanding his troops. He pushed and dragged people to their senses. One by one, they made their exits, blatantly annoyed by their host's arrogance.

Kenny checked the time. It was nearly six o'clock in the morning, and Shawn would be home by nine.

"Max, you gonna help me or what?"

Kenny felt extremely frustrated and annoyed. The cocaine he had sniffed moments ago started to magnetize his ego. "You handle that mess on the floor. I'll get you some cloths and carpet shampoo."

"Why…why do I have to clean up the vomit?" Max had been shooting heroin through his veins all night, and he was literally a moving zombie. Kenny tossed a couple of dish towels to Max, which hit him in the side of his head.

"Hey man, why you playing?" Max giggled like a silly school kid.

"Ain't nobody playing around here. So get to work and clean it up."

*****

Both Shawn and Shawn's teammate, Daniel sat quietly in the car. It had been a long and hard season. They had not done as well as expected. He was tired and just wanted to get home, take a shower, and chill out for a couple of days.

It had been two months since he'd last seen Andréa, and he was not sure whether or not to continue the relationship. He had grown to love Andréa because it seemed that she was willing to be that homemaker-wife that he had wanted. He still contemplated if the love he had for her was enough. He returned his attention to the road and the view ahead. He was happy that he was able to take a slightly earlier flight back from San Diego.

Shawn put his head back to ease the tension of his mental thoughts. As he looked out the window, he saw two women struggling to walk down a side road. Shawn looked suspiciously at them supporting each other as they futilely tried to keep their composure.

"Look at those chicks. They look ridiculous. I hope they're not coming from your house, bro." Daniel laughed quietly as they passed them.

Shawn and Daniel had become good friends in the Stallions. Daniel had helped Shawn settle into his new lifestyle as a pro football player. They trained together, hung out together, and within a short space of time, became almost like brothers.

"I almost forgot," Daniel said. "I'm going to a party tonight in Bel Air. I wondered whether you wanted to come along, chill out. You know, check out the scene."

Shawn turned to Daniel. "I don't know I wanted to just chill at home tonight."

"Oh, come on, man. It will be fun. It's kind of an industry thing. It's exclusive, too. You don't have to stay long, just come out for an hour, meet some new faces, have a drink and relax. It will be fun." Shawn paused. "All right, I'll come for one hour only."

As Daniel pulled into his driveway, Shawn grabbed his bag

from the back seat and stepped out of the car.

"So we're on for tonight then? What time should I pick you up?"

"It's all right. I'll drive and pick you up. I wouldn't want you to have to leave early. I'll come about 10:30."

"All right, Shawn, if anything I can catch a ride back with one of the guys. I'll see you at 10:30 sharp. This is gonna be interesting."

As Daniel drove off, Shawn pondered Daniel's last comment. Shawn turned to open the door and felt a slight squish underneath his right trainer. Shawn looked down and found his Nike sneaker cushioned in a puddle of vomit.

Kenny heard the car pull-up in the drive way; he peeked through the window and saw Shawn emerge from the car. "Damn, that's Shawn! Max, go and grab the stuff from the table." They both rushed over and scavenged the glass table, picking up the remaining marijuana and cocaine from the tabletop. Max tried to shove the powered substance back into the transparent packet, most of it stuck to the vomit covering his hands.

As Shawn opened the door, the pungent smell of vomit and alcohol hit his nostrils.

"What the hell is going on?" Shawn yelled, his eyes skimming over the various bottles and garbage scattered on the floor. Before crossing over the threshold, Shawn removed his vomit-covered shoe and placed it at the door step.

"Kenny—hey, Kenny!" Shawn's voice roared like a lion as he continued to walk around his house, searching for his brother. When Kenny heard Shawn's voice, he rolled his eyes and tucked the drugs into his pockets.

"What, man? What's the problem, bro?"

"What do you mean what's the problem? Look at the state of my pad. I'm getting sick and tired of this, Kenny." Shawn took one look at Max who was doped out of his head.

"Hey man, what's up?" Max asked. "You're doing your thing on the field, Hard Back Shawn and all that."

Shawn glanced at Max and did not even respond to his

compliment. He looked at him from head to toe in disgust.

"What is this fool doing in my house?"

"Look, Shawn, don't start your nagging now. You're starting to sound like a woman. Yadda, yadda, ya…"

"Do you know what, Kenny? I have had enough of you fooling around in my house. If it's not one thing, it's another."

"Oh, so you had enough now, huh? It's funny how I couldn't say that when dad was whooping my tail because of something you did."

"Oh, so because of that, it means that I should put up with your trash for the rest of my life? You're a grown man, Kenny…acting like a little kid. When are you going to grow up and be a man?"

As Kenny pulled back his hand, his fist aimed for Shawn's face, Shawn grabbed his arm and twisted it behind his back, then pushed his face against the wall.

"What are you trying to do, Kenny, huh? What are you actually trying to do?" Shawn said.

"Easy man, take it easy. We're gonna clean up this place. That's your brother, you can't kill your brother," Max said.

Shawn took one look at Max and loosened his grip. As Kenny turned around to face Shawn's intense glare, a small plastic bag fell from his pocket. Before Kenny could retrieve it, Shawn bent down and took it. Shawn narrowed his eyes, examining the substance through the bag.

"So you're a drug addict now? In my house?" Shawn stood face to face with his brother. "Clean up this place, pack your things, and get out."

Kenny had never seen his brother this furious before.

Shawn marched out of the room and went upstairs. As he reached his bedroom, he slammed the door behind him and flopped down onto his bed. A sudden surge of rage went through his body, creating a headache that made him tense all over. He could not believe Kenny. He had had enough. Right now, Shawn needed to feel some loving hands and comforting words. He got up and searched through his bag for his cell, needing to hear Andréa's voice.

With the phone to his ear, he stretched himself out across his bed and waited for her to pick up.

"Hey, you're back. How are you?" Her voice was like a caress.

"I could be much better…" Shawn said.

"So, how could I make it better?" Andrea said.

"With you coming over."

"Well, I'll check my diary, but I think I'm booked up today," Andréa responded, imitating a secretary.

"I think you may have to make a few cancellations as this is an emergency."

"Well, I'll see what I can do."

As Andréa closed her phone, she smiled. She had been praying about Shawn. She was so in love with him, but did not want to rush things. It almost broke her heart when he said he wanted time out. She paused for a moment and reflected. She saw her reflection in the mirror.

Look at me now, I am with the man of my dreams who is an established athlete, and my business is doing well. I'm gonna fix him something he'll never forget… Andrea said to herself.

Andréa smiled, went to her bedroom, and opened her closet. It had been a long time since she'd seen him. She wanted him to see what he had been missing. She pulled out a multi-colored dress and threw it on her bed. She began to scan her closet, running her fingers through the shoulder of her garments, looking attentively at the different shapes and sizes.

What does he like? Hmm, maybe I should just put on some jeans—I don't want to overdo it.

Andréa was glad that her day was free. She could completely focus on her beloved Shawn. She returned her attention to the dress she'd thrown on her bed, and picked it up again. She held it against her body and viewed herself in the mirror. The dress was an alto-neck, knee-length dress with orange, red, and browns running in and out of it. The dress was fitted and complemented her slim frame. Andréa threw the dress back onto her bed as her chosen garment, and returned to the kitchen.

She opened the fridge and took out a packet of prawns. As she began to prepare her meal of love, her thoughts ran on the intimacy of their relationship. Since her last relationship, she had been living a life of celibacy. After her broken engagement, she had suffered with intimacy issues. She had endured a season of thinking that she had turned her so-called fiancé gay. With Shawn, she felt protected, precious and priceless.

Chapter Fifteen

S hawn did not realize he had been sleeping that long until he looked up at his bedside clock. It was midday. He sat up in his bed and stretched with a yawn. He got up and headed downstairs. As he reached the living area, he looked around and was relieved that his pad had returned to its usual order. The smell of vomit and alcohol had escaped through the cracked windows. Fresh air circulated throughout the house. The house seemed extra quiet, which made Shawn feel uncomfortable. Being by himself was something he was not used to. He went over to the stereo and put on a Wayman Tisdale jazz CD. After Ria had left, he had taken on her passion for smooth jazz music.

The sound of the bass, rhythm, and sax groove began to flow throughout the room. Shawn hesitated as his thoughts ran over Kenny. Sleeping had helped him cool down, allowing his anger to dissipate as his brotherly love kicked in. Shawn grabbed his house phone in order to call him. As he picked up the phone from the glass table, he saw a set of keys atop a folded piece of paper. He lifted the paper, allowing the keys to slide off onto the glass table. Shawn opened the folded paper and read it.

To Shawn,
You're a jerk of a brother. Thanks for nothing. Have a great life. p.s. Everything you have become is because of me. Remember that!

Shawn clenched his jaw and crumpled the paper with one hand. He threw the balled up paper in the bin. He could not believe the way Kenny acted. Before Shawn could ponder on Kenny's words, the doorbell rang. Shawn walked confidently to the door, ready for round two of Kenny's Casanova special. As he opened the door, he was pleasantly surprised to see Andréa standing there. He almost forgot that he had spoken to her before taking his nap.

"Hey, Andréa."

He was impressed. He looked at her from head to toe and knew she had made an effort. He embraced her and gave her a light kiss on the lips. After the distance he had requested from their relationship, he was not as excited to see her as he thought he would be. As they kissed, Andréa hung on for more, but Shawn placed a kiss on her neck and then pulled away.

"What's this?" Shawn asked, turning his attention to the bag in her hand.

"It's your food."

"Hmm, I'm starving. What you got in there?"

"A little something for me to cook up."

"What, you got to prepare it? It's not cooked?"

"I've lightly prepared it. Don't you want fresh food?"

Andréa took the bag back from Shawn and cat-walked to the kitchen. Shawn watched as she swung her hips from side to side. He knew that she was teasing him. Shawn followed her into the kitchen like a cat after milk. As Andréa stood by the table counter, Shawn moved in behind her and slid his arms around her waist. As she felt his muscular frame behind her, she went weak.

"I've missed you, Shawn, I really have."

"I missed me, too."

Andréa chuckled. "Why are you always playing?"

Shawn smiled. "I have missed you, Andréa. I'm really glad you came over."

She turned in his arms to face him. "I need to know where I stand with you, Shawn. Are you in this for the long run because to be honest with you, I don't want to waste my time. I'd rather not be fooled again."

"Hey, where's all this coming from?"

"I just need to know, Shawn. If you are in it for the long term, then I will give you all that you want. I will sacrifice for this relationship, if it's worth it."

"Are you sure you mean that? You won't run off and leave me standing here with my heart in my hand?"

For the first time, Shawn was speaking from his heart. It seemed as though the shield he had built up had fallen down and all of his emotions were taking over. He couldn't stop himself from saying each word that proceeded from his mouth. It was as if all the pain he felt when Ria left him was pouring out. The incident with Kenny, combined with being left alone, was too much for him to handle.

"No, baby, I would never dream of doing that to you."

"I was hurt very badly in my last relationship. The woman that I thought I would spend the rest of my life with chose her career over me. We were together for seven years, since college."

Andréa took a deeper look into Shawn's eyes as her own eyes brimmed with tears.

"I will treat you no less than a king. I will pledge my life on it."

Shawn had never heard such devotion from a woman before. He was taken aback. Somewhere, somehow, he wanted to hold back a bit. It seemed a bit too soon for this type of talk. He then reminded himself of what waiting too long could do. Shawn wiped the tears from Andréa's eyes with his thumb and looked at her. He nodded to reassure himself that he was making the right decision.

"I love you, Shawn," Andréa said, her voice cracking with the words.

"I love me, too." Shawn said.

"Shawn!" Andréa playfully slapped Shawn on his chest. He hugged her tight. He loved how much she loved him. "I'm joking. I love you, too, babe."

Andréa's heart rippled on the fact that Shawn's 'I love you' was not as heartfelt as hers. And when he said it, he had failed to look into her eyes. Her last experience had taught her to be very observant. However, she chose to ignore her gut feeling of his insincerity and pushed it out of her mind. As Shawn released his

grip, he slapped Andréa's backside.

"I really am starving now, girl. I'm about to waste away."

"All right, baby. I'll have it ready in forty-five minutes."

"I'll jump in the shower in the meantime and freshen up."

Curious, Andréa looked around.

"Where's Kenny?"

"I kicked him out."

"Why?"

"I came in this morning to a dump, cans everywhere, vomit on the floor."

"What! Did he have a party or something?"

"Yeah, he did, and this is not the first time. I can't keep on baby-sitting him. And to top that off, he's doing drugs."

"Oh my goodness, Shawn." Andréa covered her mouth with her hand. "Do you know where he is or where he'll be staying?"

"No, and right now, I don't care."

"You can't tell me that you don't care about your brother."

"I've just had enough. I really have, and I'm tired."

"Tired and hungry, huh?"

Shawn smiled at Andréa. She always had calming words. It felt good to Shawn to have someone around him that loved him more than he did. He needed that support. Being alone was something he did not like.

"What about after you come out of that shower, I'll give you a soothing back rub, and after that, you call your brother to make sure he is at least somewhere safe."

Shawn hesitated. He really did not want to, but the back rub was a good persuasion. "All right."

As Shawn disappeared upstairs, Andréa whirled around the kitchen like the pro she was, rustling up a love feast for her man.

As Shawn entered the shower, he thought about how much Andréa cared for him, and not just him, but his brother, too. This made such a difference in his life, having his girlfriend and brother actually get along. As the water showered over his muscular body, Shawn felt the warmth of the shower inside his soul, lifting up his spirit. He smiled to himself.

*****

Ria sat on the edge of the couch after she had laid her newborn son in his cradle. She had called her sister to tell her of the new arrival. Ria had not bothered to tell her mother as she did not want a lecture about what a mistake she had made by moving to New York and her favorite saying 'I told you so.' Ria reclined back further into the couch and put her feet up on the footrest; she thought about names for her son. She peeped over into the cradle and looked at her son sleeping peacefully, unaware of the drama that surrounded his arrival.

Jackson Joshua Matthews, that's it.

She was convinced that the name suited her bundle of new life. As Ria reflected on the recent events of her life, she was amazed on how quickly her life had changed. From being in a 7-year relationship, single, relocating and then a mother all within a short space of time was enough to send her around the bend. But she felt strong, strong enough to combat any challenge.

Chapter Sixteen

S hawn was slightly relieved that he had called Kenny, even though Kenny had given him the cold shoulder. As Shawn put his hand to his neck, he was reminded of the back massage Andréa had given him.

He fixed his T-shirt for his night out and checked his reflection before splashing on some Calvin Klein cologne. He was looking forward to a boys' night out. Shawn grabbed his cell from the dresser and called Daniel.

"Dan, I'll be at your place in about fifteen minutes."

"All right, I'll see you in a bit."

Shawn turned out all the lights to his home, and the loneliness reentered his soul. He wanted Andréa to stay until the morning, but she refused. Seeing Andréa earlier that day made Shawn feel like he had gotten over Ria. He breathed in the fresh air as if it was a new day. As Shawn entered the car, he turned the ignition and the car radio automatically came on playing a Chante Moore track, *It's Alright*. It was Ria's favorite song, the song she used to serenade him with—and she sang it almost as well as the artist.

Shawn quickly changed the station before he allowed his imagination to get the best of him. He did not want to ruin his night out by contaminating his fresh air. He did not want to get caught up in the past. He had a good thing now, and he did not want to mess it up.

Shawn arrived at Daniel's house and blew his horn. Daniel came out and slid in the passenger seat.

"All right, bro?"

"Yeah, I'm all right," Shawn said, nodding his head.

Traci, Daniel's wife, stood at the door, moving her head to the right and left as if trying to see who was in the car. Shawn let his window down and waved a greeting. Traci looked at Shawn and abruptly turned on her heels and entered her home, ignoring his greeting. Shawn frowned and looked at Daniel.

"Don't worry, man. She's crazy."

"Time of the month thing?"

"Probably something crazy like that."

It was a twenty-minute drive to the mansion in Bel Air. The mansion was situated behind a huge gate which had a security man. Daniel said something to the security man, and the sour-faced guard allowed them access through the gate.

"This place is kinda top secret?" Shawn asked.

"A lot of celebrities and athletes come here, so the security has to be tight."

After Shawn parked the car, they both headed to the door of the mansion. Daniel rang the doorbell, and a man opened the door.

"What's up, Daniel?"

"Hey Mike, what's up?"

Shawn observed how Daniel and Mike related to each other. It seemed their eye contact had more to say than the words they said. He had never noticed Daniel associating with Mike when they played together. Shawn greeted Mike with a bit of distance in his tone. As Shawn and Daniel walked into the main room packed with men, Shawn started to feel uneasy. There was too much testosterone in the air. The room was bright with crystal chandeliers hanging from the ceiling. There were platters of food on a big oak table by a large bay window. As Shawn reviewed the room, he saw a lot of familiar faces. A man from the corner of the large bright room called Daniel over.

Shawn followed behind Daniel, feeling as though he was being watched. From the corner of the room, he noticed a man watching him in the way that a woman watches an attractive man. Shawn shot him a look and frowned.

"What type of party is this, Daniel?"

"Chill out, man, just chill."

Shawn felt even more uncomfortable in his surroundings. The atmosphere was extremely weird. Where were all the women? It felt too concentrated, too male-oriented. Shawn noticed a few of his old teammates, which eased some of the tension he was feeling. He acknowledged them with a hand signal.

"Hey Stewart, how you doing?" Daniel said, approaching one of his teammates.

"I'm well. How you doing? You're looking good, man." Stewart smiled at Shawn. "I see that you brought a friend."

"Yeah, this is Shawn."

"Yeah, I know his name."

The man smiled and stared at Shawn. Shawn smiled lightly and looked over his shoulder to avert his eyes from the man's unnerving gaze.

"Shawn, this is Stewart. He organizes these parties."

"Oh, really?" Shawn was pretty sure of the nature of these parties. He grabbed Daniel's arm. "Can I speak to you in the hallway?"

Stewart looked at Daniel and shrugged his shoulders.

In the hallway, Shawn spun and faced Daniel. "What type of gay party have you brought me to, man? What type of business are you into?"

"Shawn, relax. I felt the same way as you, but once you try it, you'll enjoy it."

"Try what, man? Are you out of your mind? You must have me mixed up with someone else. You have a beautiful wife at home and you're into this?"

"You got it wrong, Shawn. I'm not gay."

"So what are you then, bro? What exactly do you do in this party? There's not a single woman in sight, just dudes everywhere checking out dudes."

Shawn started to raise his voice, drawing attention to the hallway. Daniel tried to hold Shawn's hand to reassure him, but Shawn pulled his hand away.

"No, dude, you got me wrong. And I got you dead wrong. You ain't right, none of you are. Y'all make me sick, man," Shawn declared with disgust as he walked out into the humidity of the night. He could not believe what he had just encountered.

Even though Shawn was trying to be serious, he chuckled to himself and shook his head.

Ria would have loved this one, he thought.

Chapter Seventeen

*I*t felt strange being back in LA. Things had seemed to stay the same, but Ria felt so different. She had been in LA for only a week, and she was already on the prowl for a new home. Being back in LA caused a lot of memories to chase her, memories of Shawn. It seemed that when she was in New York, she was able to get away from the subtle reminders that pierced her heart. As she drove to the grocery store, her mind reviewed the past year's events. Now, knowing all that she knew, if she could rewind the hands of time, would she have still said yes to that editorial position in New York? Ria wasn't sure now.

Now that she would be working back in the LA office, she knew that there would be question after question about why she and Shawn broke up and her baby Jackson. Ria had done well in keeping her business to herself, and everybody seemed to know everybody's business apart from hers. But now that Shawn had become a household name, she knew that all the attention would be on her. Her life had catapulted itself into a chaotic state. She had not yet found an apartment and half of her belongings were still in New York. James had offered her an apartment in LA, but she turned down the offer. She wanted time to find the right place for her and Jackson. In her eyes, James had done more than enough in supporting her, and she did not want to take advantage of that. Besides, staying at her sister's house helped relieve her from her motherly duties.

Ria tried to clear her head from her busy thoughts. As she walked into the grocery store, she removed a shopping list from the back pocket of her jeans and glanced over it. While she skimmed through the contents of the list, she grabbed a cart by the door and pushed it down one of the aisles. Ria scanned her eyes through the shelves, and as she moved into the fruit aisle, her ears picked up on a conversation some woman was having on her cell phone. As she looked behind her to match a face to the voice, Ria observed a tall slim lady with striking hazel eyes and braids tied back into one large braid. She laughed airily and smiled like a little girl in love for the first time.

The lady came to a stop in the middle of the aisle like she was the only one in the grocery store. She seemed to be oblivious of the other shoppers moving busily around her. Every so often, she would apologize for being in the way, but she remained focused on her call. Ria tried not to stare, but something about the lady seemed strangely familiar. Ria could always remember a face but not a name. Her mind searched to place her but she couldn't. But she knew she had seen those hazel eyes before. The fact that she could not place her made Ria slightly frustrated and stare even more. As she pretended to look down the aisle, she was able to get a clearer glance.

"Okay, Shawn, baby. I'll see you when you get back...I love you, too!"

Ria's ears pricked up like a cat. Her heart skipped a beat. Ria leaned forward and squinted her eyes, looking at the woman from head to toe. Before Ria could finish scrutinizing the woman, the lady caught her staring and gave her a 'Can I help you' look.

"I'm so sorry for staring like that. I was just admiring how nice your shoes are. They are the bomb." Ria's cheeks colored as she gave the woman an exaggerated smile. "Where did you get them from?"

"The shop." The lady narrowed her eyes and pierced them through Ria before turning and walking sharply on to the next aisle.

Stuck up witch. *I know for sure that Shawn would never go for something like that.*

Ria dismissed any further thoughts about the woman and focused her attention on her shopping list as she worked her way around the grocery store.

*****

Andréa exited the grocery store, she could not believe she had seen Shawn's ex. What was she doing back in LA? Shawn had told her about Ria and how she had left him to follow her career. She knew that Ria had broken his heart and because of this, it made loving Shawn that much harder. She remembered Ria's face from college. It seemed that Ria had not changed much. She still maintained her warm smile and pearly white teeth. Even though she had put on a few pounds, it was all in the right places. Andréa wouldn't mind a little more curve to her hips and more plumpness to her derriere—listen to her, comparing herself to Ria, just as she had done back in college. Especially when Ria had started dating Shawn. It was as if she had put a spell on him. And she also remembered her last conversation with Ria, the phone call a few months back when Ria had been abrupt and rude to her.

That heifer better go back to New York and back to that rock that she climbed out from.

With jealousy flashing in her eyes as she loaded her car with her groceries, Andréa vowed that she would not allow anyone or anything to get between her and her man. Ria had her chance. Now, it was her time to shine.

*****

Tandra and Ria sat across from each other in Chanel's large living room.

"He is just so cute. I think he's got your eyes, girl. Does he sleep well in the night?"

"Nope, he gets up like three times in the night and as soon as I put him on the breast, he goes back to sleep again."

"He must definitely get that from Shawn."

They both laughed.

"So, does Shawn know about him now?"

"I just haven't had the guts to tell him. It's so hard because I think he's in a relationship now, and it seems for all this to come up, it's going to be something. I've kept it quiet for too long and to tell you the truth, Tandra, I'm scared."

"Girl, look, if you want to carry on without Shawn knowing, I will support you. But soon, when Jackson gets older, he's gonna want to know who his daddy is. And by that time, it's going to be even more complicated."

Ria lifted her eyes to the ceiling and rolled them back down again. "I know, I know. And now that I'm back in LA, I'm gonna have to face the music."

"So, what is your mom saying about it? She be loving Shawn like he's her own son."

"The usual trash that you would expect her to come up with. 'You got to tell him,' 'I told you that you should have stayed in LA,' blah blah blah…"

"She's got a point, though, Ria."

"Anyway, enough about my drama. What about you? What's been happening since I've been away? You seeing anyone special?"

"Oh, girl, nothing compared to you. And on the relationship-side, it is as dry as the Sahara desert. I just don't have the strength for it right now. The kids are getting bigger and stronger, and I have to focus my time on raising them now. It does get lonely sometimes, I can't lie, but that is the path that I'm on now. So tell me something, Ria. If you told Shawn about Jackson, and he wanted you back, would you get back with him?"

"I really don't know, Tandra. I know he'd make a good father. Why?"

"Because raising a child out here by yourself is hard work. And then trying to find a decent man who would take you and your child on is a whole different ball game. To be honest with you, if I was in your shoes, I'd be running to tell that good man that I have his child.

"I've seen him with that chicken head girl he's dating. She does not even come close to your caliber. You two are made for

each other."

"It's not as easy as that, T. He was the one who decided to break up. Things were running low in our relationship before we broke up. So maybe this is what he wanted. It surprises me how quickly he was able to move on with another relationship.

"I'm not even thinking about getting involved with anybody right now. I mean, seven years of my heart, good-loving, cooking, and my life? Right now, I'm going to concentrate on the love of my life, which is my son."

"Okay, it's your life. You know I will support you, no matter your decision."

A small silence stretched between them before Ria broke it. "I'm going to look at an apartment in Sherman Oaks. Are you free?"

"Sherman Oaks, Is James paying you that much girl, or are you giving him a little something, something extra?"

"Girl, please."

"I am convinced that he has a little something for you. There's nothing wrong with a white brother liking his coffee black—darker the berry, the sweeter the juice, and all that jazz."

It fascinated Ria how Tandra could read people like books, and how she could be so dead-on with her assumptions. "Oh, you think so?" Ria said, trying to act oblivious to Tandra's observation.

"I'm sorry, but in this world, the likelihood of a white brother giving a black sister an apartment in New York for free, and still keeping her on after he finds out that she's pregnant, girl, that's like a million to one chance. If it's not the fact that James has a little jungle fever, then you better put a dollar on the lottery. With your type of luck, you might just win it." Ria laughed. She loved having Tandra around. Any time she was feeling low, she knew Tandra would put a smile on her face.

"Anyway, I got to get back to work. I don't live a life of leisure, so I'll call you later. When are you going to view the apartment?"

Ria went over to Tandra and collected Jackson from her arms. She held him and hatched him to her shoulder. He wormed about on her shoulder, making little squeaky noises.

"I've got it booked for next Tuesday at 6:30."

"All right, let me try to see if I can drop the kids at my mother's. I would not want to bring them little terrors along."

As Ria saw Tandra to the door, she was overwhelmed with tiredness. Her week had been extremely ongoing, with settling back to LA life and Jackson getting up three times a night—it had taken its toll on her. As Ria went up to the spare room of where she was residing, she passed her sister who was sitting in her home office.

"Chan, I'm just going to have a nap. I am exhausted."

"You want me to take Jackson off you?"

"That's okay. I'll put him on the breast. He'll be a sleep within five."

"All right then, honey. Are you coping well?"

Chanel knew that her sister was going through a hard time. She had not given Ria her opinion about the whole situation with Shawn. She knew that whatever Ria decided to do would be best for her.

"I suppose so. It feels like I'm facing the world at the moment."

"You should really try to take some time out. It's only a week since you got back from New York. You have to give yourself time to settle down. Being a new mom is not easy either, Ri."

"I know Chan, but I just want to keep moving." Ria said.

Ria nodded and turned to continue her journey toward her room. After she placed her son in the center of the bed, she went to her laptop and checked her emails. From the time Jackson had turned three months, Ria had started working from home. It had kept her mind busy and helped her focus on the tiny individual she had devoted her life to.

As she sat by the small wooden dresser, she logged on her account and saw that she had ten new emails. One was from James, so she clicked on it.

Hi Ria,

I hope you and JACKSON are settling down well.

I thought I'd bring to your attention that the Ink Awards are due to happen in September. And guess what? You've been nominated for an award. I guess all that hard work has paid off. I will be back in LA in a month's time so we'll catch up then, as we'll have a few things to organize regarding the show.

Take care,
James

Ria's heart raced. She could not believe it. As tears of joy welled up in her eyes, Jackson began to get fed-up of his prostrate position on the bed, and began to cry. Ria picked him up once again.

"Hey, Jackson, Mommy's been nominated for an award!"

She positioned herself on the bed, leaned on the head board, and placed Jackson on her chest.

"It's me and you against the world, baby."

Chapter Eighteen

*K*enny sat in the dimly lit room. His friend Max was on the floor, lying on his side in a corner with his back toward Kenny. As Kenny scanned the disorganized floor, he looked for a syringe, anything to carry the fix he needed into his veins. Max had introduced him to the harder stuff. It had seemed that it did a better job of hiding the past and the pain that he felt. He now began to enter the dark part of his soul. He started to hear the tormenting voices of his past. He could hear his dad yelling at him, that he was a mistake, that he would not amount to anything. The images of the brutal beatings and verbal abuse emerged before his eyes like a movie.

"No dad, please no more. I won't do it again."

He grabbed his head, trying to stop the haunting voices. As Kenny cried desperately, he grabbed a used syringe and tightened his belt around his right arm. He just wanted it to stop. As he injected the heroin into his thick pulsating vein, he felt it flowing into his bloodstream and leaned back, content as all his torment diminished. Kenny returned to his version of normality and unstrapped the belt before walking over to Max. As Kenny shook Max, Max fell on his back from the side position he was in. Kenny jumped back and stared at his friend, his mouth ajar. Max laid there with his eyes wide open and glazed over. White foam was protruding from his mouth and nose. Kenny, not knowing what to do, looked around him and ran for the door.

Once he hit the outside world, the sunlight beat down on his eyes and entire being. It seemed that the strangers he passed were watching him. Being high, Kenny found this level of paranoia overwhelming. The unnerving feeling that someone was following him was driving him crazy. As he hurried on, he kept seeing a shadow hovering behind him. He looked back to check, then stopped and made a full circle in the middle of the street. First, he turned clockwise, then counter-clockwise, trying to catch the person who owned the shadow.

"What man, what man? Where are you at? You punk, come out and fight like a man!" Some bystanders looked at Kenny and shook their heads.

Not succeeding in finding the culprit of his own shadow, Kenny continued to walk on. Every so often, he would stop and continue the banter with himself, challenging the air that tormented him.

*****

It was a beautiful morning, and Ria was driving with her son to the Santa Monica beach. She felt fresh and exuberated. Since Ria learned about her Ink Award nomination, she was walking on air. At this point, she was not confident that she would win. The simple fact that she had been nominated kept her cool, calm and relaxed. She turned up her Usher CD playing "Simple Things"; it was sounding real good in the California heat. As the brightness of the sun hit her hopeful face, she pulled down her sun shield and pulled up to a traffic light. While waiting for the light to change, she looked out of her window. Her eyes abruptly seized its admiration of its surroundings and gleaned on a man on the opposite side of the street. He was dressed in a dusty pair of black jeans, his shirt was an off-white, and he looked worn out. She lifted her eyebrow, watching as he spun around in circles like a mad man. Ria moved her shades to the top of her head and covered her mouth with her hand. "Oh my goodness, that's Kenny." She rolled down her window and shouted, "Hey Kenny! Kenny?"

Ria tried to shout his name again, but with her being on the opposite side of the road to where Kenny was, her voice became drowned in the surrounding activity of the speeding cars that zoomed by. When she tried to shout again, a car behind her tooted, reminding her that she was at a traffic light. She drove on hesitantly, determined to get back to where she had seen Kenny. Questions ran through her mind. What happened to Kenny? Where was Shawn? Did he know about Kenny? As she turned on the road that would take her back from where she'd came, Ria's eye scanned the street in search for Kenny, but she didn't see him. She drove back up again. After four futile attempts, Ria gave up. Perhaps she had been seeing things. Perhaps that wasn't Kenny after all, just some really messed up guy who looked a lot like him. Ria shrugged her shoulders, hooked a U-turn, then headed for the beach.

*****

Shawn stepped out of the shower and strutted into the locker room with his towel wrapped around his waist. After the other night with Daniel, his mood had chilled. As Shawn applied lotion to his back, he was conscious of exposing his body. It had not mattered before, but now he was paranoid. The teammates he'd seen at the party carried on as if they had never seen him there.

This made Shawn feel awkward. He did not know whether to keep his distance or to carry on as normal. It was times like this that he missed Ria. He needed someone, a friend he could trust and confide in. He thought of telling Andréa, but with the whole situation surrounding her ex, he just did not feel comfortable bringing up the subject to her.

Naked, Shawn glanced around the locker room, watching to see if any of his teammates were checking him out. He had to man–up about the situation. It was not like him to be moved a situation like this. Shawn finished dressing, grabbed his bag and slung it over his shoulder. As he started to walk outside, he felt a tap on his shoulder.

"Hey, Shawn, I think we need to talk."

Shawn stopped and faced Daniel. He waited for him to continue.

"Look, I'm sorry about the other night. I don't want to lose you as a friend."

"You won't lose me as a friend. I'm not going to disown you because you're a freak on the down-low." Shawn smiled, easing Daniel's anxiety. "I was just taken aback the other night. I mean, what are you doing moving in those circles? You have a beautiful wife—I just can't understand. What is drawing you to that?"

"I don't know, Shawn. The excitement, the intensity, something different. To tell you the truth, Traci and I have been going through a tough time in our marriage. We have not been intimate for almost a year now. We have become like two strangers in the house. We don't even sleep in the same bed."

"Haven't you tried to talk it out, to find out why?"

"Naw, man. I can't even be bothered anymore with all the emotional stuff. Anyway, I think she knows."

"What? About the dude parties? Don't you love her? Or care for her anymore?"

"She's keeping quiet because she doesn't want to jeopardize the lavish lifestyle I'm providing her. I know that she's probably in the game, too, man. She be coming in late sometimes and talking on her phone for hours. Last week, some punk sent her flowers to my house. I told her that whatever she's doing, keep it out of my house. Bro, in this industry, it's not only on the field that you are playing a game."

"Boy, what a whole lot of drama. So what if Traci leaks it out to the press? What's gonna happen then?"

"I told you, man, she ain't gonna tell no one."

"Anyway Daniel, I've got to go. My woman is coming down, so I'll catch you later."

"So we're cool then, Shawn?"

"Yeah, we're cool."

Yeah, he forgave Daniel for luring him to a gay party, but the whole situation irritated him inside. Why would a man of Daniel's caliber be doing what he was doing? He slapped hands with his friend, then headed for his car. As they parted ways, they both knew that their friendship would never be the same.

Daniel felt better having spoken to Shawn. As the garage door opened to his home, he saw Traci's car parked awkwardly in the garage, preventing him from parking. Frustrated, Daniel hopped out of his car and slammed his car door. He stormed through the garage and entered his house.

"Hey, Traci. Traci!" He shouted. He entered into the kitchen and saw her sitting calmly behind the breakfast counter with a glass filled with ice and alcohol. She was still wearing her nightgown.

"What?" Traci said with a drunken slur.

"Your car is blocking me from parking. Move it." He stared into her eyes, waiting for a response.

"No, I'm leaving it right there. Go and park somewhere else, fool."

"Look, Traci, I haven't got time for your foolish games. So move the damn car."

Daniel walked over to Traci and grabbed her arm, pulling her to her feet. The stool she was sitting on dropped to the floor as he began to drag her out of the kitchen. She pulled back and resisted.

"Get your hands off me! Don't you dare touch me." Traci grabbed the glass of alcohol and threw it into Daniel's face. The glass dropped to the floor and smashed into pieces. Daniel, now infuriated, wiped his face with his hands and grabbed Traci again, slapping her hard across her face. The strength of the slap made Traci fall onto her back against the sink, and she slid down to the floor.

"Is that what you want me to do to you, huh?" He stood over her. "What's the matter with you, woman?"

Daniel marched off, cursing beneath his breath. He had never hit Traci before, and it scared him to see what he was capable of.

Traci slowly rose to her feet, using the corner of the sink to pull herself up. She pulled open the cutlery drawer and grabbed a huge carving knife. She looked over her shoulder just in time to see Daniel's back disappearing down the hallway. As quietly as she could, she followed him, clutching the knife in her shaky hands. Thinking about his audacity to put his hands on her, she

touched her stinging cheek and sobbed.

"How dare you put your hands on me."

Daniel turned to face her and noticed the knife.

"Traci, put the knife down. Don't be stupid. I'm sorry, I shouldn't have hit you, just calm down." Daniel stretched his hand out in a calming measure as he saw the deranged look in her eyes.

"There's a lot of things you need to be sorry for, isn't it, Daniel?"

She started to circle him, waving the knife carelessly as she spoke.

"What about the men, huh? All those men you've been sleeping with. You think I don't know about the parties you go to, you and Shawn? I should kill both of ya'll."

"Traci, I don't know what you're talking about. You've gone crazy."

"You're the one who's crazy, fool."

"Traci, look, maybe we can come to some agreement." Daniel felt exposed and scared. He never really thought that Traci knew about his double life.

"What about the agreement we made ten years ago at the altar, Daniel?" Traci sobbed. "'Til death do us part."

Traci walked closer to Daniel, aiming the knife at him. Daniel stretched out his hands, trying to determine his wife's mind. He grabbed her hand, and they began to wrestle. Traci held the knife tightly, trying to stab Daniel. Daniel jived to the left and right, avoiding the blade. Traci, still in her drunken state, put up a resistance and managed to catch Daniel off guard. She drove the knife deep into his right arm. Shocked, Daniel stared at the nine-inch blade sticking out of his arm. Traci gasped, looked at the injury caused by her own hands, then covered her mouth and started to walk backwards. She exited the hallway and ran to collect her car keys. She ran out to the car, leaving Daniel slumped on the floor, bleeding profusely.

*****

Ria looked attentively at the Ink Award's itinerary which James had emailed her. She looked through the list of nominees. Ria also looked at the other categories for best hip-hop, health, rock, and alternative lifestyle publications. Ria took a sip of her coffee and as she reviewed the sport publication nominations and who would be presenting the award. There it was in black and white: Shawn Matthews. Ria almost choked on her coffee before she swallowed it. It had been two months since she had left New York and she was yet to tell him of his son. Ria knew her time was running out from hiding Jackson from him. The possibility of her now bumping into Shawn at the awards show was high. The show was only four weeks away. Just the thought of seeing him again made her feel very nauseous. She imagined how she would tell Shawn the news at least a 100 times, and it wasn't at an awards show.

Ria took a sip of her coffee; she was determined to stay focused. "I'm gonna go and whatever happens happens. I can't keep running forever."

Chapter Nineteen

Ria had moved into her new condo, which she absolutely adored, with its three bedrooms, en-suite master bedroom, and huge French doors with a Spanish-décor finish in neutral colors throughout. Baby Jackson had grown; he was now crawling and pulling everything in sight down to his enjoyment level. As Ria sat on the carpet, she played with Jackson and smiled at his facial expression. Being a single mother was not easy, and she often found it difficult to find time for herself. Between motherhood and her career, she often felt like a robot. Settling back into her old office was harder than she'd thought. She strangely always happened to hear the echoes of whispers that bounced around the office about her quick return to LA. However, with the Ink Awards taking place that evening, Ria was too excited to worry herself with office gossip.

Ria peeked through her living room curtains to see if Cissy had arrived yet. Out of all her friends, including her sister, Ria had chosen Cissy to attend the awards with her because of her maturity and decorum. She knew that Cissy would not embarrass her with the 'Oh my goodness, there's what's his name' and 'Let me go and take a picture and sell it on eBay' attitude. Ria looked at the dress hanging on her wooden mahogany living room door. It was a Gucci dress, black velvet, sleeveless with a small train. It had three diamond trails that started from underneath the arm and circled down and around the dress. The diamonds sparkled as the breeze from the large window caressed the dress. Ria's diamante strapped shoes remained in the box, wrapped in a satin cloth. She had her hair done earlier that day—freshly washed and relaxed; it was styled up in a Sixties beehive, pressed for perfection. Curls danced atop her beehive, and a straightened bang framed her oval face.

She had spent almost $3,000 on her whole outfit, not to mention the diamante choker, bracelet, and earrings she had purchased at Tiffany's. For once, she was able to spend comfortably without thinking about the cost. Ria was not a millionaire, but she lived a very comfortable life. Exhale Magazine paid her well.

Ria looked at the time again. The clock read 3:17. Chanel would be there at four to pick up Jackson. Ria picked up Jackson and placed him in his jungle gym. As she walked away to finish preparing his bag for his overnight stay with her sister, he called to her, exposing his two little teeth. He was going to be one year old in a couple of months, and she could not believe how quickly time had passed since she had given birth to him. He already had his own personality. Ria smiled at her son. "Mama gonna be back, my suga plum."

She made a baby play-face that made Jackson giggle. Ria went to her stereo and put on a CeCe Winans CD that Chanel had given her. She had been attending Christ the Chief Cornerstone Church with Chanel. Since she started going, she felt protected, and a peace surrounded her life. The church had a single-mothers group where Ria met all kinds of women that she really connected with. Chanel's husband was the associate pastor, which allowed Ria to ask about religious things that she was not sure about. She still was not convinced about the tithing thing and being born again. One thing that drew Ria week after week was the singing. She admired the choir and longed deep down to sing, but she kept that between her and God. A few of the women from the single-mothers group encouraged her to take the step, but Ria always put it off. As Ria allowed the words of one of CeCe Winans' songs to soak into her soul, she stood still and lifted her head.

God, if you let me win this award, I promise I will start paying my tithes.

Ria smiled and laughed at herself as she continued to fold up

Jackson's clothes and placed them in his bag. The intercom buzzed, announcing the arrival of both Chanel and Cissy.

"Girl, hurry up and let us in. We want to see that banging dress," Cissy said in anticipation.

As they entered into Ria's spacious hallway, Chanel ran over to grab little Jackson who cried out when he saw his beloved aunt. He stretched out his hand to receive a big kiss and hug from her. He smiled and giggled as Chanel made baby faces and tried to communicate in his baby language. Cissy followed after Chanel, walking gracefully with a suit bag looped around her arm.

"So this is the award-winning dress? It's absolutely beautiful, Ria. Hmm, when Shawn sees you in this, honey, he's gonna drop that girl."

"Why do you have to go there? I'm over him now. I've moved on."

"Really? With little mini-me Shawn over there looking in your face for the rest of your life, are you sure about that?"

"I ain't even trying to think about that today, so can we just change the subject?"

Chanel looked on in silence, deciding not to involve herself in such a dead-end conversation.

"But you do know that there is a big possibility of you seeing him there? You do know that, right?"

Ria walked off into her room, ignoring Cissy's comment. She really did not want to think about it. She just wanted to enjoy the day without thinking about any difficult situations. Cissy followed her.

"All I'm saying is that you need to prepare yourself."

"Prepare myself for what, Cissy? Look, Cissy, please can we just drop this conversation? You better not go on about this all night; otherwise, I will just go by myself."

Trying to pour water on the potential flame, Chanel now joined the conversation. "Anyway, Ria, I must say I am really proud of you, girl. You are doing your thing."

"Thanks, Chanel. I should have taken you with me instead."

"All right, all right, Ria," Cissy said. "I apologize. I did not mean to go on about it, but you know, I just think that the way you're going about the whole situation is wrong." Ria shot Cissy a last chance look, which ceased Cissy from continuing her rant.

"Ria, look, I better be on my way," Chanel said. "Have you got Jackson's bag together?"

"Yeah, it's right here. I didn't pack too many diapers. I think I left a half pack at your place."

As Ria passed Jackson's overnight bag to her sister, Ria's phone rang. She went to her night stand and picked it up. "Oh hi, Mom, how are you?" Ria looked at her sister and sarcastically rolled her eyes.

"Ria, just a quick call to say that I wish you the best for tonight. And despite what you might think about me, I only want the best for you. You are my last born."

"Yes, Mom, I do know that, but sometimes I just need your support and encouragement. You have to leave me to make my own mistakes."

"I know, baby. I just don't want to see you hurting because it kills me to know that you are hurting. You're a mother now, so you'll soon understand the emotions I go through. Anyway, how's my grandson?"

"He's waiting for you to come and see him. He's gonna be one very soon."

"Well my sixtieth is next September. I was thinking of coming down to spend it with you guys. Anyway, I got the pictures you sent. He looks more like you than Shawn..."

Ria laughed.

"So have you heard from Shawn, baby?" Sharon asked cautiously.

"Why would I have heard anything from him?" Ria responded sharply.

"Well, not stating the obvious, but you have his chi..."

"Mom! Chan wants to speak to you," Ria cut Sharon off. She refused to have another conversation about Shawn tonight.

Chanel could tell by Ria's expression that Sharon had said something that Ria did not like. As Chanel took the phone, Ria took Jackson from her and put him on the carpet so that he could crawl around in her bedroom. Ria walked toward her large mirror and looked at her reflection. Even though Ria was annoyed by her mother, the truth was her mother was right and Shawn had a right to know. Ria promised herself that she would tell him that night. Even though it was not the ideal setting, carrying the burden was too much for her to carry.

Chapter Twenty

The hall was grand with chandeliers hanging from the ceiling. The chairs were arranged in theatre-style. The stage had white satin curtains hanging from each side, and the pillars throughout the hall also had white draped curtains flowing with bits of glitter.

"I really can't believe I'm sitting here," Ria said in slight awe.

"You better believe it because it's real. This is not a dream at all."

"Cissy, I just really can't believe it. Never in a million years did I think I would be able to achieve this success. You are probably used to all of the glitz and glamour, but to me, it's like a whole new world."

"A whole crazy world," Cissy said with a smile. "Thanks for inviting me to share this experience with you. You could have chosen your sister, but you chose me, which touches my heart. I didn't mean to go on earlier, but you are like my little sister, and I feel that I have a responsibility to ensure that you make the right choices."

"I know, but let's just enjoy the night."

"When are they going to announce your category?"

"I'm not sure. To tell you the truth, I really don't mind if I don't win tonight. I haven't been an editor for long, and to be nominated for an award is enough. Maybe I'll get it next year."

"Girl, stop with all that modest stuff. We are seated in the fourth row. So doesn't that mean anything? Only winners sit up in the front."

"Well, I did say a little prayer earlier on. I said to God that if I won, I would start paying my tithes." They both chuckled quietly as the hall began to fill up.

"I'm sure half of that tithe is in your whole outfit, girl," Cissy remarked while snaking her head like a diva. They both laughed again.

As the ceremony started, different editors and personalities descended up and down the stage to collect their awards. To break up the boredom of the winners' speeches, different music artists performed their hit singles. As Ria's nominated category came up, she froze in her seat. She tried not to look too excited as the camera was on all the nominees. She held her breath slightly while Cissy held her hand. Ria squeezed it. There was silence as the presenter, a well-known supermodel, opened the envelope. Ria exhaled with disappointment; she didn't win. Ria felt Cissy's other hand softly rest upon her hand. She turned to her and whispered into her ear, "Oh, girl, I'm sorry. I really thought you had a chance."

Ria found herself entering her auto-pilot mode and heard herself say, "It's okay. It really is okay. Like I said, maybe I'll get it next year."

As the winner approached the stage, Ria clapped and falsely smiled. Ria took a bit of tissue from her small bag and dabbed her face slightly. Well that was one heart attack out of the way, Ria thought. Let me prepare myself for the other. "Ladies and gentlemen," the announcer said, "we would now like to announce the award for the best sport's publication of the year. Please, let us welcome Shawn Matthews from the Stallions."

Ria's heart began to race. She could not stop her heart from pounding. Get a grip, girl. You're over him, get a grip. She was in complete anticipation.

As Shawn strode onto the stage, his lean stature encouraged a few whistles from the seated females. Cissy turned to look at Ria, but Ria kept her eyes on the center stage.

With one hand against her diamante choker, she watched Shawn intriguingly. He looked handsome and strong. Her heart began to beat hard, which filtered out to her chest. She took deep breaths in, trying to control her emotions. Had Shawn spotted her from the crowd? She was so overcome by the moment that she could not even hear what he was saying. As Shawn opened the gold and black envelope, he reviewed the name on the card and looked out at the audience, scanning quickly to see if he could see the winner. Ria wondered whether Shawn had seen her; she was so close.

Seeing Shawn in the flesh had knocked all her senses out of joint. As Shawn and the winner disappeared off the stage, Ria's air passage felt tight. She needed some air. She collected herself and nervously rose from her seat. "I'm just going to the restroom."

"Okay, you want me to come?"

"No, no. I'll be back."

"Are you sure?" Cissy asked, concerned.

"Yes." Ria took a deep breath and began to walk up the aisle.

Each step she took made her feel like she had bricks in her strapless pumps. As Ria reached the back of the huge hall, she entered into a corridor that had a few people networking with each other.

Ria continued toward the ladies' bathroom, and she saw her rival winner gleaming with happiness. The winner was a curly blonde Caucasian lady. She had the appearance of a human Barbie doll, plastic all over. Ria mentally rolled her eyes and took a deep breath before transitioning into the actress role she found herself playing from time to time.

"Hey, congratulations. You deserved it, well done. Anyway, see you at the after party." Ria winked and smiled before she swiftly moved on. She did not wait for her rival's response, but felt her rival's eyes pierce through her back as she hurried toward the restroom. She entered in and glanced at the eight cubicles and black marbled floor, which was shined to perfection as if it were a sheet of crystal glass. The atmosphere was scented with different types of perfume flowing in the air, which was a bit overwhelming for her. She cleared her throat.

With only two ladies occupying the wash basins, puckering

their lips and powdering their faces, it was strangely quiet. They briefly observed Ria as she came in, then returned to their gossip as if they'd never seen her. Ria approached a cubicle and checked her small diamante bag for her cell phone. She entered in the neat, small, and spotless stall and placed the marble toilet seat down before sitting. Ria flipped through the phone book until she got to the P's. She stopped at Pastor Joseph. Ria pressed the call button and awaited a response.

"Hello Pastor Joseph speaking." She hesitated. "Hi Pastor, it's Ria."

"Hi Sister Ria, how are you?"

"I'm okay, Pastor."

"Are you sure? You don't sound okay. What's the matter? Is something bothering you?"

"Well, it really is nothing, Pastor. Just the usual drama I seem to get myself into."

"You want to talk about it?"

"Well, you know I was up for an award tonight?" Ria said.

"That's right, the editor of the year."

"Yeah, well I didn't get it, and I saw my ex for the first time in almost a year and a half. Pastor, when I saw him, all these emotions came up from inside of me that I thought I had gotten rid of. And the worst part is that I still haven't told him that I have his child. I don't know why I have let this issue consume me so much. I'm trying to get my life straight now and be a good mother to my son, but I may not be doing him any good if I am denying him of a father." Ria said.

"I see. It sounds like you're really going through it. One thing I know is that you are a very good mother. Even though this seems like a difficult time right now, God will see you through it. Emotions are funny things. They are tied to the soul. And when you have been with someone emotionally, intimately, and then share a child together, you are tied in those areas and it is hard to untangle yourself out of it. Is that making any sense to you?"

"Yes, Pastor." Ria responded.

"It's going to take time and a lot of prayer, which means you

do have to get serious with your Christian walk in order to receive your full healing and strength from God, Ria."

"What about telling him about our son? I think that he is in a relationship now. What if he rejects his son and does not want anything to do with him?"

"Sister Ria, speaking as a father, he has the right to know that he has a son. Even though it might be rough at first, you will feel relieved when you take that bulk off your shoulders. But take note, Ria, when you do break the news, be open to his reaction, and know that it may not be what you expected. Try to see it from his point and give him time. And that award you did not get, sister, your award lies in heaven. You don't need people's approval, only God's approval. Amen?"

"Amen, Pastor. Thank you. I really was not sure who to call, but I'm glad that I called you."

"Praise God. Is there anything else you want to talk about?"

"No, Pastor. I will see how I get on with this one before I rail out the rest."

"So I'll be seeing you this Sunday?"

"Yes, bright and early."

"Blessings, Sister Ria."

"Blessings to you, too, Pastor."

Chapter Twenty-One

As Ria put her cell back in her bag, she felt so much hope, and the anguish that she felt moments ago had disappeared. Ria stepped out of her cubicle and was greeted by an African-American, middle-aged woman who had jet black hair cut into a small afro. She wore a glittery silver dress, which complemented her beautiful dark ebony skin.

"Hi, how are you?"

"I'm fine, thank you." Ria said walking up to the mirrored wash basins and rested her handbag atop the counter.

The lady followed her. "I must say, you have such a beautiful dress on."

"Oh thanks. It does a good job in hiding those bumps and lumps I can't get rid of." Ria responded.

"I saw that you were up for the editor of the year."

"Yes, but I didn't even get it."

"The fact that you was up is an achievement. It's very rare for an African-American, nevertheless a black woman, to be nominated in this industry."

"Yeah, I guess." Ria said flippantly. The lady paused and glared at Ria.

"You know, you should be really grateful because back in the Sixties, black sisters…" As the lady began to rant on, Ria blocked out everything the lady was talking about. As to not appear rude Ria would acknowledge what she was saying with a *that is so true*. She did not want anything to disturb her peace. Ria opened her bag and pulled out her transparent MAC lip-gloss. She dabbed it on her lips, then puckered them together. She quickly gave herself a once over by doing a half turn in the mirror.

"Thanks for that encouragement. I really needed it. I must get back, I've left my friend out there. See you later." The lady was slightly startled by the interruption. "Ur okay, take care."

Ria grabbed her opened bag, clutched it under her arm, and left.

"Phew, what a headache," she whispered to herself. She was now ready to enjoy the rest of the show. As she walked, the bricks that she once felt attached to her shoes had now disappeared. This encouraged her to walk with graceful confidence and her head held high. As she walked, she failed to notice the small raised step before her, which made her trip slightly. Her bag fell to the ground, scattering all its contents. Just when she thought she had gotten herself together, her bag had to let her down.

"Enjoy your trip?"

She looked behind her to that so familiar voice and saw Shawn standing, smiling at her, locked and mesmerized by her beauty. Ria smiled as she removed one of her curls from her face. She made every effort to keep her cool.

God, I need more of what you just gave me back then, like right now, Ria pleaded before responding, "I did, thanks. I'll remember to take you down with me next time."

"Make it France next time." Shawn said and stepped closer, Ria was not sure how to greet him. A lot of time had passed since they had been together. Ria's brain flicked through what was appropriate. *Should I hug him, shake hands, hug and kiss, jump on him?*

Shawn walked closer. Ria stretched out her hand to shake his, unsure of his response. She saw that Shawn could see her awkwardness, and he took her hand and gently drew her to his chest. Ria wrapped her arms around Shawn's shoulders, felt his warm embrace. She gripped him firmly between her arms. She almost forgot about her cosmetics scattered on the floor behind her.

"Well done, Miss Jackson. I'm proud of you."

Ria loosened her grip. "Proud of what?"

"What you stood for and what you have achieved."

Ria stared into Shawn's eyes. She saw how much Jackson looked like him. Her stomach knotted. Hearing those words from him was to her better than any award she could have won.

"Thanks, Shawn. That means a lot to me."

Ria held onto Shawn's hand as his presence gave her butterflies. She remembered how those strong hands used to hold her at night. She was not only holding the former love of her life, but the father of her child. As they stood there, gazing at each other, the silence between them said so much about how they felt about each other.

*****

Andréa looked on from the entrance of the main hall, seeing all that was going on between Shawn and Ria. She spotted Ria when she first stepped into the auditorium with Cissy. There was no way Andréa was going to allow history to repeat itself again. Things had just started to settle between her and Shawn, and she did not want anything to rock the boat. She had let down her entire guard with Shawn, and they both had become intimate with each other. Andréa had previously vowed to herself that she would hold out until she got married, but having Shawn in her life had persuaded her to throw out the promise she had made to herself and God.

Andréa continued to stand there, observing all that was going on. Her blood boiled inside as she saw Shawn's expression to his ex-lover. Her hazel eyes narrowed, intensifying her focus on Ria. If looks could kill, Ria would have dropped dead, right there on the floor.

Shawn could not quite put his hand on it, but he felt connected to Ria. Deep down in his soul, there was a tugging. Seeing Ria in the flesh brought back emotions that he had tried to suppress while being with Andréa.

"You look absolutely beautiful tonight, Ria. I must say, you've put on a few pounds, though." Shawn grinned at Ria while observing her shape.

"Oh you really think so, huh?" Ria could not help but encourage Shawn's flirting by turning a little bit more so he could see her full silhouette.

"So what's been happening?" Shawn said.

"This and that. I've moved back to LA, which has not been easy. What about you? How is football, Mr. Hard Back, or whatever they call you."

Shawn chuckled. "So you've been watching me then?"

"Well I-I may catch a game or two when I have time"

"Well, being on the team is great, but the industry is crazy, man. I've got stories upon stories to tell you, Ri. Anyway, I'm glad you moved back to LA. New York is too fast and too cold. I've been praying that you would come back ever since you left."

Ria looked at Shawn with one eyebrow raised and a smile on her lips. "I guess your prayers have been answered." Ria said flirtatiously.

"Well, I do attend church now and again for a little spiritual enlightenment. It's good for the soul." Shawn said.

"That's a funny thing because I've also been attending church, and you're right about that enlightenment thing. It helps me get through the drama of life. So, are you seeing anyone?" Ria could not help herself. It was if her mouth had a mind of its own.

"Yes, I'm seeing someone. But that does not stop me from missing you. You were a big part of my life."

Ria allowed Shawn's last sentence to sink into her heart. If only he knew how bigger a part of her life he was. Once again, they got caught in each other's gaze.

"So, how's that relationship going? Are you happy?" Ria tried to break the intensity that was starting to build up between them.

"It's going all right. So are you...in a relationship? Seeing anyone special?" Shawn really did not want to know, but he felt he had to ask.

"Well, I do have someone special in my life."

"Oh really. I would like to meet him one of these days."

"Hmm." Ria said nervously.

Shawn looked around the room to hide his disappointment. He hated the thought of her wrapped up in another man's arms.

"Anyway, you truly look so beautiful tonight, Ria. And whoever he is, is a very lucky guy."

Just before Ria could respond, an attendant approached them.

"Excuse me, Mr. Matthews, There's a lady named Andréa Lasalle, asking for you. She wanted you to know that she is ready to go home.

Ria could see from Shawn's hard sigh that he was annoyed.

"Yeah, she's with me. Could you ask her to meet me here?" Shawn said.

"No problem sir."

"Thank you."

As the gentleman left to attend to Andréa, Ria began to feel nervous. She had never been in this type of situation before. She was not sure how she would respond seeing Shawn's girlfriend. Would she be slightly jealous and show it? Or would she be nonchalant, acting as though their relationship did not faze her?

"I better get back to my seat. Cissy is gonna wonder where I've gotten to." Ria said trying to make a quick exit.

"You're here with Cissy? How is she?"

"Oh, she's fine. You know, doing her singing thang." Ria tried to escape again.

"How's your mother and Chanel?"

"They're all good." It was too late. They both turned toward Andréa as she approached them. "Hey, I wondered where you got to, honey," Andréa said as she kissed Shawn on the lips, without acknowledging Ria. Shawn held back slightly, the awkwardness of the situation was making him tense. It was a striking contrast between the relaxed mode he was in with Ria.

"Andréa, this is Ria, my urr…"

"Friend. I'm his old time friend. Nice to meet you." Ria felt immensely uncomfortable seeing another woman kiss Shawn.

"Yeah, you too," Andréa said flatly.

At that moment, Ria recognized Andréa's face from the grocery store. As Andréa and Ria's eyes met, they both recognized each other.

"Anyway, it was nice to meet you, Andréa. And it was really good seeing you again, Shawn. We must all catch up for dinner sometime." Ria said.

Shawn looked at Ria strangely. It was as if Ria had changed into a flight attendant, her posture and speech had altered completely. As Ria reached her hand out to shake Shawn's hand, he squinted his eyes at her, questioning her sudden change. He pulled Ria close in an embrace, and whispered in her ear, "Meet me here after the show, okay?"

"All right," Ria said quickly. The fact that he had done that in front of his girlfriend made her feel very edgy. She had never had to fight over a man before, and she wasn't about to start now. Ria scanned the floor for her cosmetics, picked up what she saw, and walked back to her seat. Shawn watched Ria depart to her destination.

*****

Andréa could not believe the coldness Shawn had shown to her. She looked at him sternly. "So what was that all about?" Andrea said abruptly.

Shawn took one look at Andréa and saw how mad she was at him. "Look, Andréa, don't start."

"What do you mean don't start, you have just disrespected me in front of that woman. What's your problem?" Andrea said feeling the blood run fast through her body.

"Look, I tell you what, Andréa. I think we better call it a night." Shawn clinched his jaw and walked off, leaving Andréa standing there by herself.

"Shawn?"

"I said we better call it a night." He said and disappeared in the same direction as Ria.

The harshness of Shawn's voice took Andréa aback. She was hurt that the man she adored and loved could talk to her in that way, especially in public. She considered doing two things:

popping Shawn in his mouth or telling him that it was over between them. She was fed up of the mood swings he constantly put her through.

*****

"Girl, I was about to send out a search party for you. What happened? Are you all right?" Cissy whispered.

"I think so. I bumped into Shawn."

"What? Oh my goodness, I knew you would. So, what did he say? What did you talk about?"

"Well, just the casual stuff, nothing deep. He wants me to meet him after the show." Ria said.

"What? May I ask what for? I think this is the best time to talk about Jackson." Cissy stated.

"Cissy, what is this, The Spanish Inquisition?"

"No. I can see that you really do love him. I can see it all in your eyes. Look at you, looking like a lost puppy."

"Cissy," Ria said defensively. She paused. "I think you're right. It's hard for me to face that fact. But I also have to face the fact that he has moved on with his life too. He has a girlfriend now, who I actually met." Ria said leaning back more comfortably in her chair.

"What? All of this happened while you were out there? Oh my goodness, so what does she look like?" A man sitting behind her tapped her shoulder to inform her that she was talking too loud. Cissy apologized sincerely before she returned her attention to Ria and maintained her quiet, but excited tone. "So what does she look like?"

"She's all right. Tall, slim—I wouldn't say that she's ugly, and I wouldn't say that she is overly attractive, but she's just okay. The funny thing is I've met her before in Walgreens. She caught my attention because of her striking hazel eyes, her face was also familiar, but I could not place where I had seen her. I thought it could only be a coincidence when I heard her mention Shawn's name."

"You're kidding?" Cissy responded.

"I knew she recognized me as well. I could see it in her eyes." Ria said.

"That must have been awkward. How did Shawn introduce you to her then? Did she say anything about meeting you before?"

"No, she kinda gave me that look."

"What look?"

"That type of look that says he's mine and don't even think about it." Cissy found it amusing.

"looks like you got yourself a little competition where you may need to grease your knuckles and take your earrings off, gurl." They both chuckled lightly.

"That's not even funny. I would not fight for a man if my life depended on it. But just to let you know, I'm a descendant from the islands. I will split her in two." They both laughed again childishly.

After they had finished laughing, there was a small silence between them, and then they returned their attention toward the stage.

Ria turned to Cissy. "I'm scared," she said. "I'm scared about how I feel, telling him about Jackson, scared of his reaction."

"Look, don't worry. It is a difficult situation, and the longer you leave it, the worst it will become. Even if you never get back together with Shawn, at least give him the opportunity to be a good father to his son. Isn't that the most important thing? And the way this industry runs, it's better that you tell him than for him to find out from a tabloid newspaper. Now that would be a shame."

"I know Cissy, I'm going to sort it out tonight."

"Well, you know what? In the words of your sister, go in the power of His might."

Chapter Twenty-Two

*Q*s people started to slowly leave the auditorium, the silence was broken with mutters from different parts of the hall. Ria turned to Cissy and took a deep breath.

"Well, here goes. He better not leave me standing there any longer than five minutes—actually, he better be there already waiting."

"Girl, calm down, relax. You don't need to get an attitude about it. We don't want it turning out to be baby mamma drama, and I look too good to be fighting anybody tonight. I have a hundred and fifty dollars in a form of a hair style that's gonna have to last me a week and—"

"Cissy! I get the point. You know me better than to be fighting over any man. You should know me by now."

"I'm just warning you. Women change when they bear a boy child. Anyway, you want me to wait for you?"

"Yes…actually, no. If anything, I'll get one of the attendants to call me a taxi."

In silence, they walked side by side through the auditorium doors and down the corridor. As Cissy stepped ahead of Ria, she looked around to see if she could see Shawn. Ria nervously tried to keep her eyes on her footing because she did not want another free trip. Cissy slightly turned her head and whispered, "He's over there, on the right."

"What?"

"I said he's over there, on the right."

Cissy waved at Shawn when he took sight of her. Ria kept her view on the floor. Already her body was crawling with anxiety. The floor seemed like a safe enough place to look.

As they walked closer to Shawn, they found him engaged in a conversation with a white lady.

"You did not tell me that his girlfriend was white," Cissy whispered.

Ria tore her eyes from the floor and glanced in Shawn's direction. "No, that's not her. The girl he introduced me to is a sista," Ria said.

"So who's that white girl with him then?"

"I don't know. Do I look like his keeper?"

Not anymore girlfriend, Cissy thought.

Already, Ria's emotions were making her feel a bit edgy, and Cissy's constant questions were beginning to annoy her.

"Oh my goodness! How are you, Shawn? It's been a long time since I last saw you," Cissy said excitedly. They greeted each other with a kiss on the cheek and a friendly hug while Ria stood behind Cissy like a shy school girl.

After the exchange of pleasantries, Shawn signaled with his eyes that he needed to be alone with Ria, and Cissy gladly stepped back, exiting the conversation.

"Anyway, I better be off. I'll leave you two love bir—ur…I mean…"

Ria gave Cissy the 'you better leave now' look before she rolled her eyes and pretended to perfect the back of her hair with her fingers while looking around the room.

Cissy's awkwardness showed as she bit the side of lip. "You guys have a good night. I'm sure you have a lot to catch up on." She raised her eyebrows at Ria before she kissed both Ria and Shawn goodbye.

While Ria and Shawn watched Cissy disappear into the crowd, Shawn turned to Ria. "Let's get out of this place. I'll get my driver to drop us off at my house—if that's all right with you."

Ria tried to respond, but got locked in Shawn's deep eyes. She could not quite get her head around the fact that she was looking into the face of the man who fathered her child.

"Ye…Yeah. That's fine, Shawn."

As they stepped outside, the California air was sweet and warm. Ria absorbed her surroundings and found it difficult not to get carried away by the atmosphere and the mood of things; it relaxed her slightly.

You'd better get it together, girl. This is not the time to be falling in love again. Remember, he broke it off and left you, Ria coached herself in order to stir up the attitude that Cissy had warned her about.

"So, where's your girlfriend?"

That's right, girl, keep the convo on the girlfriend that he got with, moments after he finished with you. Ria thought.

Shawn turned to Ria as they walked through the back door toward the parking attendants. "I sent her home."

"You sent her home, just like that?"

"I told her I had some business to tend to."

"Sounds like you've got her wrapped around your little finger."

"Come on now, Ria. You know that I don't have little fingers or feet for that matter." Shawn grinned.

Ria tried to act serious, but could not help but be a little amused. "Well, excuse me," Ria said, not knowing how to respond.

"You're excused, baby."

Ria shook her head while she smiled.

"Some things just never change." Ria slapped Shawn on his broad shoulder. Ria slid into her side of the car as Shawn waited for her to grab the tail of her dress before closing the car door. He then hopped in on the opposite side.

Girl, you better tell him that no old time's sake hanky-panky is going on tonight. Ain't nothing going on but the child support. You're a church girl now.

Shawn stretched his hand over the back of Ria's seat so that his hand reached the back of her head rest. Ria could not help but steal a few glances. He'd unbuttoned the top of his shirt, exposing his muscular neck. His body had become more defined and leaner than she had remembered. It was as if her eyes were magnetized to Shawn's. As she tried to apply her attention elsewhere, she could not help but take a second look, then a third look, until she got caught.

"I must say, Shawn, you look very well and healthy. Have you dropped some pounds?" Ria asked as naturally as she could muster.

"You think so? The training regime is quite intense. I guess you get out what you put in." Shawn became strangely quiet. It was like he wanted to say something but was reluctant to do so.

Ria could see his internal struggle. "Shawn, what's wrong? You want to say something?"

"I was just thinking…nah, it's all right."

"No, no, what is it? Just say it."

"Nah, it's probably not appropriate to say…"

"Shawn, just say it, and I'll tell you if it's not appropriate."

"I was just thinking it's a shame we did not…"

Ria hated when Shawn paused in a sentence. Every time he paused, it meant that it was something that really bothered him. "Have any children. It takes a long time to reach that point in a relationship." Shawn said.

All Ria could do at that moment was an ambiguous hum. "Well…I think we have very good careers now, and good memories together, and we should concentrate on what we have now, which is building a good friendship, right?"

"A friendship, huh?" Shawn said with disappointment. "Maybe you're right. It might have made things more complicated."

It was as if a dagger had gone through Ria's chest. *Okay, it's not the end of the world. I will tell him when we get to his home. I don't want the driver knowing my business.*

The driver stopped outside Shawn's residence, and Shawn helped Ria out of the car. She saw the full view of his beautiful home.

"Nice pad." Ria said.

"You think so?"

The limited conversation between them put a taste of

awkwardness in the air. Shawn walked slightly in front of Ria, leading the way. Shawn took his keys from his pocket and opened the front door. He turned on the light switch, which softly lit up the passage way and sitting area.

"Please, make yourself at home."

"Do you mind if I take off my shoes? These pumps are beginning to pinch my little toe."

"Yeah, go ahead, relax."

Ria bent down to untie her straps, Shawn went over to assist her. "Here let me help you with that."

"Oh, thanks. That's very sweet of you."

"I really don't understand why women like to wear shoes that are too small for them. It's a mystery." Shawn said.

"Let me educate you a little bit now! I buy the right size of shoes, but after a while of wearing it, especially these types in the heat, your feet swell. Does that make any sense?" Ria smiled, like she had said something clever.

"It's gonna have to." As Shawn bent down before Ria to untie her shoe, Ria felt a flow of ease throughout her body as the tightness of the straps around her feet loosened. She stepped down from the three and a half inch pumps.

Shawn held her hand to help her balance as she freed each foot from the shoes. They were now standing very close to each other. Shawn bent his head to meet Ria's lips, and their lips lightly touched before Ria pulled away.

"Shawn, we can't."

The guilt knowing that she was not totally truthful with Shawn was eating her up inside. She also did not feel right in her soul. As much as she wanted Shawn in her arms, she still remembered what Pastor Joseph had said about being serious with God.

"We need to talk, Shawn. I've got something to tell you, which I should have told you a long time ago. I think we better sit down."

Shawn took Ria's hand in his and drew her to the couch area.

She licked her lips. "I really don't know how to tell you this, and I don't know how you are going to react, but..." Shawn's house phone rang. "It's okay, leave it. Carry on."

As it continued to ring, it distracted Ria and broke down her confidence. "You better get that, Shawn. It could be an emergency."

Shawn stretched over to the glass table and picked up the cordless phone. "Hello?" Shawn's eyes widened. "What? Are you sure it's Kenny Matthews?" He nodded and added, "I'm coming right now."

Shawn's composure had completely switched from cool and calm to confused and dismayed.

"That's the hospital. They're saying that Kenny's in serious condition." Shawn grabbed his car keys and headed for the door as Ria grabbed her shoes and her little bag and followed after him. Bare foot, she walked briskly to the garage. They entered the car, and Shawn pulled out quickly, driving without his seat belt. He then pulled the belt and clicked it into place as he drove.

"You know Kenny is a drug addict," he said. "I had to kick him out the house. I haven't seen him for months. Now I get a call saying that he's in hospital..."

Ria's mind flashed back to when she thought she'd seen Kenny in the middle of the street, acting like a mad man. She squeezed her swollen feet into her pumps.

"I tried to help him, man, I really tried. I paid for him to go to best rehab clinic in California. He dropped out three times. I don't know what else to do."

Ria rested her hand on his thigh. "Shawn, it will be all right. No matter what the situation is, we'll get through it. You've done what you can do."

"It's been tough, Ria. I've had to cope with this alone. My father's a waste of space—he might as well be dead."

Ria kept her hand on his thigh, listening silently as she comforted him.

"You know how hard it was for me when my mother died? I can't go through that again..."

"I know, Shawn. Let's not think about that right now. Let's wait until we get to the hospital."

*****

As they pulled into the hospital's emergency parking lot, Shawn jumped out of the car and ran toward the reception area.

"Kenny Matthews? Can you tell me where he is? I was called and told that he was here."

The lady behind the reception desk checked her computer. "He was in intensive care. I will let the doctor know you are here. Please take a seat."

"What do you mean take a seat? My brother was in intensive care, and you're telling me to take a seat? I want to see him. What floor is he on?" Shawn slammed his fists on the woman's desk.

"Excuse me, sir, if you don't calm down, I'm gonna have to call security."

Ria took Shawn's hand and pulled him aside. "I know you're anxious, but it's better if you stay calm, honey."

The warmth of Ria's aura brought him comfort. He kept hold of her hand and took a seat in the dreary waiting room hospital.

A short, round man came down the hallway toward Ria and Shawn.

"Mr. Shawn Matthews?"

"Yes, what's happened to my brother? What's going on?" Shawn said anxiously.

"Please, could you step into this room, sir?"

Ria stood with Shawn to follow, but the doctor's questioning look at her presence stopped her.

"She's my partner," Shawn said.

His partner? With all the mixed feelings rushing through her heart and mind, Ria felt that his statement was slightly inappropriate. However, due to the severity of the present situation, Ria quickly dismissed her thoughts and refocused her energy on supporting Shawn.

They entered the room, the doctor closed the door behind him.

"Mr. Matthews, it seems that your brother had a drug overdose. We have been able to stabilize his state, and he is out of intensive care, so he should be all right. The only complication we have is his health insurance coverage."

"Don't worry about that, I'll cover that side of things. So he'll be all right?"

"He'll be fine, but he seriously needs to go into rehab if he wants to stay alive."

Shawn sighed with relief. "Thank God. Can we see him?"

"Yes, Mr. Matthews, if you would like to come this way."

Ria noticed that some of the color had returned to Shawn's face. As they entered the room, she viewed Kenny in the bed. He turned to face them as they walked toward him. Kenny looked small, frail. His bloodshot eyes revealed his drug habit. Shawn was taken aback by Kenny's appearance and shook his head as he walked closer to his brother.

"I can see that noose around your neck again, bro," Kenny said with a croaky tone and a slight smile as he watched Shawn walk in with Ria. Ria looked at Kenny with slight annoyance, but stayed by the doorway of his room.

"This is not the time to joke around, Kenny. Look at the mess you got yourself into. You're coming back to stay with me. As soon as you get out of this place, you're going to rehab and you aren't leaving there until you are off that junk. I can't risk losing you."

"All right, I'm going to try this time."

"No, Kenny, you can't just say it. You've got to mean it."

"No, I'm being serious. I don't even know what happened. My body just started to shake, and I thought I was having a seizure. There was this pain in my head—it was hell. All I knew was I woke up in this place, and I was scared."

Shawn knew that Kenny was serious. Kenny looked at Ria standing at the door and almost undressed her with his bloodshot eyes. The hairs on Ria's back spiked up.

"What you doing back there, Ria? You guys went on a date or something? You're all dressed up."

"We met up at an awards ceremony," Ria said.

"You can come in, Ria. You don't have to hide behind the door with your fine self."

Ria smiled slightly and walked up closer to Kenny's bed and stood beside Shawn.

"You are in so much trouble, Kenneth Matthews," she said while wagging her index finger for emphasis.

"I hope the trouble I like."

Ria ignored his slimy comment.

"Anyway, I'm glad that you're okay. We were very concerned about you."

"I'll be all right. I'm a survivor like a lion in a jungle."

"Or a cat that used eight lives and only has one left," Ria said.

"You see, bro, that's what I'm talking about. I lay here on my death bed and your girl is insulting me."

"That's not an insult, Kenneth. I am just telling you some home truths. You need to straighten up and fly right. I'm only saying this because I care. I don't take any pleasure seeing you lay on a hospital bed, all right," Ria said, vexed.

"Look, we are just relieved that you are alive," Shawn said. "And Ria has a point. You need to get a hold of your life. It's killing me seeing you like this."

Shawn looked into Kenny's eyes with deep concern. "I've got to sort out the insurance now, and then take Ria home. I'll be back in the morning to pick you up, all right, Kenny?"

"Make sure you just drop her off, and no taking her back home to talk."

Ria turned to Kenny with a smug grin as they both headed to the door. "Kenneth, I'm actually staying at Shawn's, so I'll be seeing you when you come out of the hospital."

"Shawn, bro, she is not serious, is she? Remember you got a woman, a good woman, that loves you and cooks you gourmet meals."

Shawn rolled his eyes and shook his head as he followed Ria out of the hospital room.

Chapter Twenty-Three

*A*ndréa rolled onto her back for the eighth time that night. She could not believe how Shawn had treated her in front of Ria. That evening had been like a bad dream for Andréa, and her mind kept replaying the whole scene. She connected the betrayal she felt now to the pain her ex-fiancé had put her through when he announced that he was gay at her Thanksgiving family reunion.

How dare he, just who does he think he is? Andréa said, raging at the air.

Every time she thought about how Shawn had treated her, a charge of rage went through her body. Her mind became so consumed with the image of Ria and Shawn that she began to feel sick. She began to mutter to herself while tossing and turning.

Andréa flung back the purple satin comforter and pushed herself up into a sitting position. She rested her back against the leather headboard. She gazed around her dark room and the fixtures that were silhouetted by the outside street light. Andréa stretched over and switched on her Tiffany lamp.

This is ridiculous. Get a grip, Andréa. He's just a man.

But I love this man.

But how could he have treated you like that? He has never done this before in front of another woman. Maybe he just had some important business to attend to. I can't be in all his business. He's not in all of mine.

She got out of her bed and took a quick look at her clock. It was two o'clock in the morning, and she had not slept one bit. She marched to her kitchen like an army soldier. Andréa grabbed a glass from her cupboard and ran the tap. She slammed the glass down on her kitchen counter before her eyes turned to a bottle of Crown Royal a client had given her.

It had been a long time since she had alcohol. Since becoming a Christian, she never had the urge to drink alcohol. She considered the water again and ran the tap, then quickly eyed the Crown Royal again. As the water ran from the tap, Andréa's body began to shake. She could not believe that she was getting so worked up about it. But she could not control herself. She desperately needed to do something to calm herself down.

That jezebel better understand that she's in for a helluva night if she thinks she gonna get her claws back into my man again. Andrea said to herself.

Andréa grabbed the bottle of Crown Royal and opened it. Before she could reconsider her actions, she felt the heat of the alcohol burn down her throat into her chest. Andréa took a deep breath and closed her eyes briefly. She leaned back on the kitchen counter. She looked up to the ceiling and hesitated, then proceeded to walk back to her bedroom in a calmer manner.

As Andréa entered her bedroom, she climbed back into bed in a solemn mood. Even though she was calmer, she felt troubled inside. It was moments like this that she would have prayed. It had been months since she had attended church or even prayed. She could not believe that she had allowed Shawn to become her all in all. As Andréa lay on her bed alone, her mind began to play images of her and Shawn spending time together, the good times. Remembering made her heart soften. She remembered the times when Shawn made it clear to the other women that pursued him that Andréa was his main interest. Why had she gotten so worked up about the whole situation? If Shawn was not in love with her, why was he telling the world that she was his special jewel?

Maybe I'm not loving him enough. Maybe it's time that he met my parents, then he will know I am serious.

Andréa became quiet within herself and pulled her purple satin comforter back over her. She lay on her side this time and reached over to turn off her lamp.

It's time for me to get serious with this thing. It's time for me to become Mrs. Matthews before someone else steals the crown. *As the bible says, it's better to marry than to burn.*

Andréa closed her eyes, for the first time that night, it seemed that the pro-Shawn advocate won the campaign, and completely took her over.

Chapter Twenty-Four

The night was calm, and a small breeze blew through Ria's side of the car window. It was a total contrast to when they had entered the car to go to the hospital.

"Let me take you home. I've had you out late enough. Where are you living now?"

"Not too far from where we were staying. I'm in Sherman Oaks now."

"Sherman Oaks. Nice, you've always wanted to live there."

"It's nice and calm. The neighbors keep to themselves. It's a bit of a distance to travel into downtown, though."

"What is it, an hour each way?" Shawn said.

"Yep, it can even be stretched to an hour and a half. Most days I'm sitting in traffic, listening to my smooth jazz, which helps pass the time."

"You might like to know, I've really grown to appreciate that jazz you love."

"Really? You always used to tease me about it."

"I've even got a few CDs."

"Are you serious? What CDs you got?"

Keeping one hand on the wheel, Shawn stretched to the small compartment on his door and took out a CD case.

"Let me see, Wayman Tisdale, Norman Brown…"

"Are you sure that's not from my collection? I swear I'm missing a few CDs." Ria said amused.

"Naw, I bought these, baby. They're all new. Do you have Norman Brown's latest one?" Shawn said.

"Actually, I don't." Ria said.

"Take it. You can have it." Shawn said.

"Thanks. I almost forgot how sweet you are. I'll think of you when I play it."

"Oh really now? You call me when you get thinking, all right?"

Ria laughed. "Oh yeah, what if I call you up and your girlfriend picks up the phone?" Ria said.

"You tell her you want to speak to big daddy." Shawn said.

"You get her to call you that?"

Shawn smiled with a grin that emphasized his jaw line. "You know what it's like. She can't help herself."

"Oh please. Well the next time I see her, I will give her the true Hollywood story of being with Shawn for seven years. So how long have you guys been…going out?"

"Not that long. Maybe, a little over a year." Shawn said.

"Okay, I see." She paused. "Are you in love with her?"

"Are you checking to see whether you still have a chance with this smooth operator? I'm in high demand now." Shawn said.

"It's not that at all. I'm just curious. I don't want to get in the way."

"You do know that curiosity kills…"

"I knew you were going to say something like that."

Ria didn't feel completely comfortable talking to Shawn about his girlfriend, but she just wanted to know.

"What about you staying at my place until later on? It's already three, and by the time I drop you off it will be close to four. We're only a couple of minutes from my place now."

"I suppose it makes sense." Ria said. Taking up Shawn on his invitation would give them more time to talk.

"I'll give you one of my old T-shirts to put on. I'm sure I still have the ones that you used to wear. Some of the stuff you left is still packed up in my closet."

"You still kept some of my stuff?"

"Well, I couldn't just throw it away. So what were you trying to tell me earlier?" Shawn curiously asked.

"I'll tell you when we get to your house," Ria said looking at her feet.

"You got me in anticipation now."

Ria's stomach knotted up again. This was it, no turning back. She had no way of getting out this time. Shawn parked in his garage and stepped out of car. He walked around to where Ria sat, and watched with amusement as she attempted to squash her foot into one of her shoes.

"I'm still convinced that women buy their shoes one size smaller than their actual size."

Ria gave up and abandoned her shoes, deciding to walk bare foot. Shawn took her in his arms and lifted her onto his shoulder.

"Oh my goodness, Shawn, put me down. You can't manage me. Oh my god!"

"Girl, you have put on a couple of pounds. What have you been eating?"

Ria hit Shawn on his broad back, then gripped tightly onto it. For a split second, she had a flashback of her and Shawn fooling around. She remembered how good that back was to her. Ria quickly snapped out her sinful thoughts; she needed no distractions.

As they reached the door, he released Ria, gently lowering her to the doorstep, and unlocked the front door. Ria walked in first, and Shawn followed her.

"Does your girlfriend know that you're this mischievous?"

He smiled at her as she sighed with relief; being on the ground kept her mind grounded. She fixed her dress, which was slightly hitched up around her thighs.

"It suits you."

"What, me being terrified?" She said.

"No, the extra pounds. It's added to your curves. It must be good living."

"Yeah, something like that," she said flatly. She could feel Shawn's eyes studying her as though he was in an art class. "So the living area is which way? My feet are killing me," Ria said, breaking Shawn's fixation on her body.

They entered into the sitting room, and she took a seat as Shawn walked into the kitchen.

"You hungry?"

"I was, but I can't eat anything at this time of the morning."

"You sure? I can rustle up something quick for you."

"What do you have in mind?" Ria asked curiously. Shawn had never offered to cook for her in the past.

"A little fruit salad."

"That sounds nice. It's light."

Ria followed him into the kitchen, holding one side of her dress up so she wouldn't trip over it.

"What fruits do you have?"

"Well, I got some pineapple, peaches, grapes—and I know how you love grapes."

"I'll just have a few," Ria said as she leaned onto the counter.

"Okay, I'll bring it over to you. Go sit down and relax and rest those swollen feet."

Ria went back to her seat, while Shawn watched her. He envisioned what things would be like if they had not broken up and they were coming home as a couple. He took a cluster of grapes from the fruit basket Andrea had prepared and picked them off the stems, then placed them in a small, round red bowl. Shawn felt butterflies in his stomach as he glanced at Ria again. It felt so right for her to be in his home. The whole scene felt like déjà vu, and even though they had just reunited, the distance he once felt before they'd broken up had ceased. This feeling of happiness and contentment was something he had not felt in a long time, ever since they had parted ways. Shawn walked toward Ria, where she sat admiring his décor. He handed her the bowl of ruby red grapes.

"Something is missing here," he said. Ria looked questionably at Shawn and plunged a huge grape in her mouth. "What?" She said.

Shawn raised one of his eyebrows and walked over to the media system and turned it on. As the bright colors illuminated the silver system, a mixture of reggae and jazz flowed through the air like a sweet aroma.

"Kirk Whalum," Ria said acknowledging the artist, "I am very impressed."

"You know, I always try my best. Anyway, what is it that you wanted to tell me?"

Shawn sat close to Ria and watched her slowly place the bowl of grapes on the glass coffee table. The look on Ria's face made Shawn's anxiety levels rise. She took his hand gently into hers and when he realized that her hands were shaking, his anxiety became fear.

"I really do not know the best way to tell you this, and I would have chosen to tell you sooner, but I was scared." Ria took a deep breath before continuing. "Shortly after I left for New York, I found out I was pregnant."

Shawn's heart stopped. He looked deep into her eyes, watching every movement of her face, but remained quiet and still.

"I had—or should I say, we had—a baby boy. He is almost a year old now." Ria stopped and prepared herself for the worse. Shawn freed his hand from Ria's and held it to his jaw. As silence fell between them, smooth jazz simmered in the background.

"So you're saying that I'm a father?" Shawn clenched his jaw. Ria nodded.

While Shawn tried to comprehend what he had just heard, Ria reached for her small diamante bag, took out her purse, and handed Shawn a small photograph. Shawn took the picture from Ria and studied it. He could not believe that he was looking at his son, his creation.

"He's beautiful. He looks a lot like me. So what's his name?"

"Jackson James Matthews." Ria said.

Shawn reviewed the picture of his son and shot Ria a look that made the hairs on her back stand.

"I can't believe it, all this time I had a son and you did not tell me. I didn't even get the chance to name my own son. You know how important those things are to me? You knew the pain I went through with my own father. Couldn't you even consider that? Where is he now?" Shawn demanded.

"He's with Chanel. You can see him later on today when I go

pick him up—if you're ready, that is," Ria said while carefully placing her hand on his right leg.

"Of course I'm ready. Why didn't you tell me the moment you found out you were pregnant?"

Ria felt uneasy as more tension entered the room. "I was scared, Shawn. I tried to tell you the time we first spoke, when I arrived in New York. But when you said you had been picked up by the Stallions, I thought it would ruin things for you. I didn't want to burden you by coming back. It would have been complicated."

"What do you mean, complicated? All you had to do was come back to LA, Ria."

"It's not as easy as that, Shawn. I did what I thought was best for both of us. Anyway, I was already in New York trying to start my life over." Ria could see Shawn's irritation.

He got up from his seat, and his face was like the calm before the storm. "Good for both of us? You mean good for you. How could you be so selfish, Ria? You made a decision that involved me missing out on the most important experience a man could have."

"Shawn, let me explain."

"No, let me finish. You let me miss out on my son being born from the woman I love, the woman I considered to be my wife, my best friend. You knew how much I wanted to have children with you."

Ria jumped to her feet, like a lawyer defending her client. "Don't pin this all on me. Remember, it was you that ended this relationship—it was you, Shawn, not me. Do you know how much you hurt me? I had no option but to just get on with it by myself." Ria said.

"I ended it only after you decided to run off to New York, with no thought to me or how it would affect us." Shawn said.

"What was I supposed to do, just stay and compromise the opportunity of my life? No, Shawn I did what I thought was best for all of us."

"Look at what that opportunity cost me. The fact that you

ended up back in LA, isn't that telling you something? You should not have gone you should have stayed."

Ria lowered her voice and regained her composure with tears. "I stood by you for seven years, remember that? I would have come back, Shawn, if you had not ended our relationship. You don't know how much I wanted to share this experience with you."

"Why did you wait so long to tell me? I remember the time I came to New York. I called you to go out. You said you had the flu or something. Why didn't you tell me then?" Shawn's tone was calmer.

"The time I wanted to tell you, I found out that you were in a relationship. Time just went by and…"

"And so, how could that had stopped you from telling me that you were having my child? Come on, Ria you've got to come up with something better than that to convince me. Because I'm having a really hard time accepting your excuses."

"Shawn, you were so quick to jump into another relationship. I really thought that you did not want me. It seemed you got over me so quickly, and I was struggling with coming to terms with the whole thing."

"But this is not about you. And that seemed to be the problem in our relationship. Did you ever think about what was best for our son?" Shawn said.

His words hit her like a ton of bricks making it hard for her to speak. Tears streamed down her cheeks. She looked Shawn in his eyes, in an attempt to plead for mercy for the guilt he was putting her through. "I know I screwed up. I know there is no excuse good enough to explain why I did what I did, but I refuse to be made the blame for our relationship. If you wanted me as your real wife, you would have asked long before leaving a ring for me on a dresser. Don't put our relationship ending solely on my back. That I will not accept."

"So you thought you'd get back at me, and punish me because I tried to move on? What makes you think that someone I just met would ever replace what we had? You should have known that I would have dropped her if I knew you were carrying my child.

You must have known that?" Shawn said.

"If I had known that, don't you think I would have just come back, Shawn? You are missing the fact that we had problems between us even before I planned to take the position in New York." Ria wiped tears from her face, smudging her eye shadow and mascara around her eyes. "Look, the most important thing, Shawn, is how we can be the best parents to our son."

Shawn grew silent as he turned his back toward Ria. "I want to see my son. Put your shoes on and get yourself together." Shawn grabbed his car keys from the coffee table.

"Shawn, it's almost four o'clock in the morning. Can't we just wait a couple of hours?"

Shawn turned swiftly to face Ria as he walked toward his front door. "You have allowed me to miss out of too much of my son's life already. I'm not missing a moment more. Get yourself together. I'll be waiting in the car. Just close the door on your way out." After Shawn's sharp statement, he marched out of the room while grabbing his car keys in the hallway.

Ria sat there, mentally and emotionally exhausted. She pushed her feet into her shoes and tied them up. She grabbed her bag and reluctantly limped on swollen feet to the door. As she closed the door, she looked up to the sky which was now allowing the sun to break through. She wished she could fly up to the sky and hide behind the clouds.

Before stepping toward the car, she called her sister on her cell phone. The phone rang almost ten times before a croaky female voice answered the phone.

"Hello, Chanel speaking."

"It's me. I'm coming over to pick up Jackson."

"What? Now? He's sleeping, the whole house is. Can't you wait until later?"

"Chanel, I told Shawn and he wants to see his son now. So, I'll be there in the next hour or so." Ria ended the call. She was not in the mood to give a further explanation to Chanel. Ria wanted the whole thing to end.

*****

Shawn sat in the car, impatiently tapping the wheel with his index finger. He felt betrayed and confused. He now looked at Ria in a new light, a light he did not like. It seemed that the woman he thought he knew was a total stranger. He kept on questioning why Ria had kept this from him. Shawn started the ignition once he saw Ria approaching the car. She opened the door and sat down down.

Ria tilted her head back against the headrest and closed her eyes. If she pretended to sleep, perhaps that would prevent Shawn from asking her more difficult questions that she was unable to answer.

Chapter Twenty-Five

It was a very quiet drive to Chanel's house. Shawn was surprised that Ria was able to sleep through the whole drive. There was more that he wanted to ask her. He wondered whether she would have told him if he did not invite her to his house. On the flip side, Ria's silence allowed Shawn to think about fatherhood. He had so much mixed emotion that he did not know whether to be happy or sad.

Shawn pulled into Chanel's driveway, and Ria stretched and yawned before opening the car door. Shawn followed her to the front door. It had been a long night and none of them had gotten any sleep. Ria knocked lightly with the door knocker, aiming not to wake up the whole house by ringing the doorbell.

While they waited for Chanel to answer the door, Shawn looked at Ria from behind. He noticed that her once so tightly curled hairstyle had lost its perfection. Shawn's heart raced as he heard baby noises through the door.

Chanel opened the door, and they entered.

"Morning," Chanel said awkwardly with slight sarcasm.

"How's it going?" Shawn said bluntly.

The atmosphere was tense. Ria signaled a look to Chanel without Shawn seeing her, which communicated her discomfort about the whole situation. Chanel widened her eyes in response. As they walked toward the sitting area, Jackson came crawling out into the hallway, as if he had sensed his mother's presence. When he saw his mother, he began to call for her. Ria went over to him and picked him up as he reached for her.

"All right, all right. What's all the tears about, baby? Mommy's here now."

Shawn watched his son and Ria in amazement. He could not believe he was looking at his son. He also could not comprehend that the baby he was looking at was half of him. Shawn walked close to Ria, and she surrendered Jackson over to his father.

"Oh, what's the matter, son. Don't cry. Daddy's here now."

As Shawn comforted his son, he struggled to hold his emotions in. He entered the sitting area and sat on the leather couch with Jackson in his arms. Strangely enough, Jackson started to settle and stare at the man that was now holding him. Shawn smiled at his protégé and kissed his forehead. Shawn perched Jackson on his knee and stretched over to pick up his Barney doll that lay next to him. Shawn wiggled the doll in front of Jackson, but Jackson ignored the Barney doll and continued to stare at Shawn with fascination.

He reached out his little fingers to touch Shawn's chin. As he touched the tip of Shawn's face, Shawn pretended to eat Jackson's little hands. Jackson let out a slight giggle in amusement before proceeding to touch Shawn's face again. Shawn once again nibbled on Jackson's hands, and Jackson giggled again.

Ria half-heartedly smiled as her sister turned to her and tapped her softly on her arm. They went into the kitchen, leaving Shawn and Jackson in the sitting room.

"You want to stay until tomorrow?" Chanel asked. "You look exhausted, Ri."

"Urh no, I don't have any clothes here to change into. I also have work tomorrow, so the sooner I get myself back into a routine, the better."

A small silence filled the air before Chanel broke it. "You must be relieved. And it's a good sign that he's taking an interest in Jackson," Chanel said trying to encourage the distressed state of her sister.

"I guess so, but I'm still very anxious about what's going to happen from now on. It seemed that I had everything under control, but now I have to put everything into God's hands and

believe that He will get me through this web of mess."

Chanel was slightly taken aback by Ria's statement. She had never heard Ria speak like that. She stretched over to her sister and embraced her. "It's going to be all right, girl. Weeping may endure for a night, but joy comes in the morning."

Chapter Twenty-Six

The room was lightly lit from the sun that peeked through the cream satin curtains. The sun almost illuminated every dark spot in the room and imitated an atmosphere of peace. The piles of clothes scattered around the room on the floor was a complete contrast to how the room looked only a few months ago. In front of the King-sized mahogany bed was a large mirror which was seven feet in length, four in width.

Daniel stood in front of the mirror, looking at his bare chest. He ran his hands over the top of his chest and down to his arm, over a large scar that protruded from his smooth, almost perfect skin. As he felt the wound that Traci had inflicted, he reflected on his life. Where had it all gone wrong? Daniel had been in recovery since Traci had stabbed him. He was unable to play football, which left him depressed and full of regret.

Daniel eased onto the end of his bed, still looking at himself in the mirror. It seemed that all his so-called friends had dropped him. The down-low partners and lifestyle simmered down like a fire being put out by an extinguisher. The party invitations seemed to get less and less, and Daniel found himself alone, feeling useless and a waste. It was as if he was a ghost, and no one seemed to acknowledge him anymore. He began to realize the mess and tragedy he had brought himself into. He was in love with the wrong things and the very thing he should had loved and cherished was gone. He remembered a cliché he used to say: if you play with fire, you're going to get burned. Right now, he felt like he was in flames, burning away in hell.

Daniel glanced at the watch on his wrist and saw that it was 8:30. Too early in the morning to be up with nothing to do. He stretched back onto his bed and closed his eyes, trying to block away the loneliness and regret he felt inside of him. As he lay on his bed in his khaki pajama bottoms, he thought about Traci again, this time in a better light. He began to reminisce on when they first met, and how much in love they used to be. He knew that Traci had been staying at her mother's house in Crenshaw because the bank statements to their account reflected where Traci was making her withdrawals. How could he make things better? How could he regain the life he once had? He hated where he was at now. He had never been alone before in his life, and he was finding it hard to deal with.

While he lay on his back, he wondered whether to call Traci. They had not spoken since the incident, which made Daniel less confident that she would speak to him if he were to call. He picked up his cell phone and scrolled down to 'wife cell.' He pressed the call button, not knowing what to say or how to say it. The phone rang and Daniel's heart upped its pace. Suddenly, the ringing stopped as if someone picked up the call, but there was silence on the receiver's side.

"Traci, Traci? It's Daniel." There was still silence, but Daniel knew that Traci was on the other side. "Traci, we need to talk. I...I was hoping we could meet up and discuss a few things." Still no reply.

"Look, Traci, I'm not mad at you. I deserved what you did. I know now that I shouldn't have treated you the way I did. I was a jerk."

"You really hurt me," Traci began, "and I don't know what good can come of me meeting with you. I'm trying to get on with my life, and I'm trying to pick up the pieces of what's left of my life."

"Please, Traci, I'm begging you, I just want to see you. I miss you."

Traci hesitated again. "All right, but you better promise me that you're not going to lie to me about the things that happened in our marriage."

"I won't, I promise. Everything out on the table this time."

"All right, I'll be around…"

"Okay. Thank you. What time will you be coming?" Traci ended the call.

Daniel felt relieved since he knew that Traci agreeing to meet with him was a good start. He glanced around the bedroom and realized the state it was in, the state the whole house was in. He began to get up and clear it, but then he stopped. He'd just leave the place as it was so that Traci could see what state he was in and living in. Maybe that would get him a few pity points. He desperately wanted his life back, and he would do whatever it took to get it.

Daniel went into the shower and cleaned himself up. He shaved his face in the style that he knew Traci preferred. He was determined that he would not let her go until she came back to him. In Daniel's heart, he knew that Traci was his last attempt of getting a life.

*****

Andréa pulled her thick duvet from over her as she heard her doorbell ring. She quizzed herself on who it could be as she struggled to pull herself from her cozy sleep. As she walked toward the door, she wiped her face with her hands in an attempt to remove any sleep debris from her face.

"Who is it?" she cautiously called out with a croaked voice.

"It's me."

Andréa let out a silent scream of shock and joy as she heard his deep voice.

"Okay, Shawn, hold on a minute."

She ran into the bathroom and quickly swallowed a small amount of mouthwash and checked herself in the mirror before sprinting back to her apartment door. Andréa quickly composed herself before she opened the door.

She looked at Shawn as he stood leaning against the door.

Andréa's plan was to play hard to get, but when she looked into Shawn's eyes, she knew something was seriously wrong.

"What's wrong, baby? Come in."

Shawn entered and Andréa followed behind him. As she closed her door, she noticed that Shawn still wore his suit from the night before. Something had to have happened. And more than likely, it probably had something to do with that girl Ria.

"Why are you still in your suit from last night?"

Shawn sat down down on her couch, but Andréa remained standing. Shawn's unexpected appearance had erased any traces of tiredness.

Shawn stared straight into Andréa's hazel eyes. "I have a son."

"Excuse me, I didn't get that. What did you say?" Andréa almost swallowed her tongue. She hoped this was his idea of a joke, but she knew that Shawn was not the type to make a joke so early in the morning.

"I found out today that I have a son." He said.

"With?" She said.

"Ria." He said quietly.

Andréa felt nauseous at the mention of Ria's name. "You've got to be kidding me, Shawn. What…when…how did you find this out? And how do you know she not lying and just wants you back? Are you sure it's even yours?"

Shawn bit his lip while he watched Andréa animate her anger in front of him. "he's mine."

"So when did this happen, huh? Huh?"

Shawn remained calm. "It was way before we met, before she left for New York. She told me after the awards last night."

"Oh, so was that the business you had to tend to?" Andréa asked. Shawn remained quiet. "I knew that woman was up to something. I could see it in her eyes." Andrea said while seething with anger.

They looked at each other, and Shawn stood and walked over to Andréa and held her waist. She continued standing with her arms folded in front of her.

"Baby, I'm sorry I had to bring you into this, but I still need

you in my life. I apologize for treating you the way I did last night. I know this is not what you signed up for, but I really need your support on this. There's so much going on right now, and I can't face it alone."

"But what about Ria? Are you sure she's telling the truth? You might want to get a DNA test. Women these days are so desperate."

"I saw him, and he looks just like me. Anyway, Ria's not the type to lie about something like that."

"But what type of woman would keep something like that from a man she supposedly loved?"

"I'm still trying to come to terms with it myself." Shawn said.

"So where does that leave us? I saw the way you looked at her last night. I cannot stand to be hurt again, Shawn."

Shawn cupped Andréa's face. "You have no need to worry about anything happening between me and Ria. The only thing I am interested in is having a relationship with my son. I care about you. If I had no interest in you, what would make me come down here to tell you that I have a son?"

Though he was pleading his case, Shawn knew deep down that Andréa was not going anywhere.

"Okay…okay, but if I am going to commit to you at this level, Shawn, I also need a commitment from you." Andréa waited for Shawn to catch on to what she was implying.

Shawn showed reluctance. "You know you mean the world to me. That should be enough. Surely you don't need a piece of paper to show that I am committed to you." Andréa shook her head.

"No, Shawn. If I'm going to play an active role in your son's life, then I have to be more than just your *girlfriend*." Andréa steered Shawn dead in his eyes until his blink broke the intensity.

"You want us to get married?" Shawn paused. Having someone was better than having no one. "All right, let's get married. If that's what it takes for you to take me seriously," Shawn said. Andréa's eyes lit up like a child in a candy shop. She kissed Shawn and hugged him close while she jumped up and down like a game show contestant. As Shawn held her in his arms, he felt unsettled by the decision he had just made, but he pushed it to the side and blamed his sudden anxiety on the night's events.

When Shawn loosened his grip on Andréa's waist, he felt completely drained. "I'm gonna lie down. I need to catch some sleep before I pick up Kenny from the hospital."

"You go ahead, baby. Make yourself at home. I'll join you later."

Shawn walked off solemnly into Andréa's bedroom. He glanced around her room and noticed that he never felt at home when he stayed in her apartment. He wondered if he had gone straight home as his gut told him, would he have saved himself from an awkward situation. Something about the whole marriage thing with Andréa made him feel uncomfortable. He wondered whether to go back and tell Andréa that he needed time to think over it. When he compared both Ria and Andréa, Andréa seemed more committed to him than Ria was. Shawn concluded that it was a good decision to have Andréa in his life. It was no longer about him anymore. He realized that every choice he made would not only affect him, but his son, too. That was the only thing that brought joy to his heart, he was a father and he would do whatever it took to make sure his son never experienced the childhood he or Kenny had.

Shawn was so tired now that he could not contend with anymore drama. As he laid his back onto the bed, he drifted out of his battling thoughts and fell into a peaceful sleep.

*****

Andréa stood in the middle of the kitchen, her heart racing as she tried to keep her feelings in check and under control. She was slightly confused, but excited at the same time. It was more than she had bargained for, finding out that Shawn had a baby with Ria. She questioned the authenticity of whether he was the father of Ria's child. If Shawn was truly the boy's father, why had Ria waited so long to tell him? There were still questions Andréa wanted to ask Shawn, but she knew now was not the right time to play detective.

She tried to concentrated on the better part of her news but her mind would not let her. Andréa stood before her open refrigerator, she reasoned with herself about the insecurities she now faced in their relationship. A baby between Shawn and Ria meant that Ria was always going to be in his life. This annoyed Andréa, and she wondered why Shawn had chosen her over Ria. Having a child by the woman would have been an acceptable reason for him to choose Ria if he wanted to get back with her.

Andréa removed two eggs from the fridge and placed them on her table top. It was not the ideal situation Andréa had envisioned for her future. But she was willing to make that sacrifice.

Chapter Twenty-Seven

$\mathcal{J}$raci drove up to the doorway and did not attempt to use the garage she once used to occupy. She slowly stepped out of the car and walked calmly toward the doorway. She rang the doorbell and bit her lip in anticipation. She look around and was surprised to see the grass, which used to be kept neat and trimmed, now growing yellow and out of control. Before she could do any further inspections, the door opened. She and Daniel greeted each other with a polite, but uncomfortable hello.

As Traci walked in, she was shocked by the untidiness of the house. She found herself stepping over clothes that were tossed carelessly on the floor. She looked into Daniel's face and noticed that the smooth complexion he once had was covered with razor bumps and worry.

"Do you want a drink or something?"

"No thanks," Traci said as she looked further into the untidiness of the house she once lived in.

"Are you sure I can't get you anything?"

"No, really I am fine," Traci said, unimpressed with Daniel's hospitality.

Daniel nervously took a seat opposite Traci, and his eyes questioned her all black attire. It was if she had just attended a funeral. He glanced at her face. She looked worn out and stressed.

"First of all, I just want to thank you for agreeing to meet me. I appreciate it." Failing to get a response, Daniel continued. "Traci, I'm sorry that I have put you through hell. I'm willing to take responsibility for everything, including the downfall of our marriage. I asked you to come because I really want us to work things out if possible." Traci continued to listen. She kept her composure cool.

"I was wondering whether we could just start fresh and put all this stuff behind us."

"How do you think we are going to that, huh? Do you know what you put me through? I could have killed you. You almost turned me into a murderer."

"I know, Traci, and I'm sorry. Since you've been gone, I've realized how much I need you. Please, Traci, let's start over. You're all I got." Daniel knelt down before Traci and took her clenched hands into his. Traci tried to pull her hands away as her eyes welled up with tears.

"No."

"Traci, please, I love you. I need you in my life. I promise you, no more lies, no more partying. We will be like we used to."

"I can't, Daniel. You've slept with men. How can I trust you again? If it was with another woman, then maybe we could stand to have a chance, but…"

"Where did you get that nonsense from, about me sleeping with men? It's not true."

"So you're saying you were never unfaithful throughout our marriage?" Traci asked sarcastically while taking her hand from Daniel's to wipe the tears from her eyes.

"To be honest, I was not completely faithful in our marriage, but I never slept with any man. That's messed up." Being truthful to Traci was not on the agenda for Daniel.

"So you're trying to tell me that I made it all up in my head? I must be crazier than I thought I was."

"Traci, please, I'm begging you on my knees. If you are not in my life, then there's no point in carrying on. Since you've left, I've been depressed. I miss looking at your beautiful face."

Daniel stroked Traci's face with his hand. This time, Traci did not resist. It had been a long time since Daniel had been that affectionate to her, and she liked it. She still loved him and missed him. Daniel was the only man Traci had ever been with. She had dedicated all of her adult life to loving him unconditionally. The

strong resistance she once had seemed to be melting away. She hated herself for it. She hated being this vulnerable.

"I promise you, baby, no more lies. Just me and you. We'll even start going back to church and getting the help we need to make this work." Daniel was silent, waiting for Traci to answer. He peered into her teary eyes.

"It's gonna take a lot of work for me to trust you again, Daniel."

"Yes, yes, I am willing to do all the hard work needed to make this work, baby, I promise you."

Traci looked at the surroundings as Daniel kissed her hands. How would she be able to continue being his wife after all she had been through? She knew that he was lying about sleeping with men, but living a lie seemed to be better than living alone with nothing. She searched his eyes for sincerity, but there was none there. Traci knew she was making a mistake, but she had worked too hard to end up divorced like her other friends.

She would hold on to the faith she had left in order to keep her marriage. The time she had spent without Daniel had given her time to refocus and think about her spiritual journey. She looked at Daniel again as he bent his head down on her lap. The one thing she yearned for throughout their marriage was a child. They had tried earlier on in their marriage, but to no avail.

"Daniel, one thing that would help this marriage work is if we really looked into having a child. That means us both going to see the doctor."

"Yeah, baby, I was just about to mention that. I know how much it means to you. Once you get settled back here at home, we'll start trying again."

Traci searched Daniel's eyes again for a hint of sincerity, and once again she saw the same counterfeit appearance, which was a typical trait that Daniel morphed into. She silently promised herself that this, she would not neglect her faith. She realized that she needed the faith of Abraham and Moses to cross this Red Sea.

Chapter Twenty-Eight

*A*dapting to her new office in Los Angeles, Ria sat behind her new desk minus the en-suite. The phone was hooked on one side of her shoulder. Like many conversation with Tandra, she could tell where this one was heading. Her main focus was on a page which she was yet to sign off, which was hitting close to deadline.

"… about seven thousand dollars to get this to work." Tandra said.

"Seven thousand dollars! I'm sorry, Tandra, I really can't lend you that type of money."

"Girl, I really need you to believe in me on this. I'll be able to pay you back when the ball starts rolling."

"What if the ball never gets rolling? I have never seen you do hair before, let alone open up a hair salon."

"I told you I would employ the hairdressers, and I will just manage it. I also wanted to attach a training program for young girls and train them so that they could have an opportunity to do something with their lives."

"It sounds like a good idea, but I don't think you have thought things through properly. Sounds very risky. Have you tried getting a business loan at the bank?"

"I can't. My credit is so messed up and…" Tandra said.

"and you want me to lend you money. No, girl, I can't."

"So you're saying that you won't lend me the money?"

"I'm sorry, Tandra. I can introduce you to possible sponsors when you get started. I have a child to think about now. I can't just throw away money like that."

"I can't believe you, Ria. I thought you out of all people would understand what it's like to achieve a dream. You have no idea how hard I'm trying to provide a secure future for my kids." Ria was getting bored with the conversation and wanted to end it fast.

"Do you even have a business plan, Tandra? I can't give you seven thousand dollars like that. I think maybe you should continue to work, get your credit straight, and review the whole thing in a year's time."

"I have already given up my job to pursue this, Ria."

"What? Are you crazy? You can't be doing stuff like that in this type of economic situation. How are you going to survive?"

"I will manage like I always do. I'm a survivor. You know what, Ria? I really admired your strength when you decided to move to New York, and I was inspired. But it seems that now you're getting paid thousands of dollars a month, you've become conceited and don't want to help anybody. I tell you what, Ria. I'm gonna do this thing with or without you. I thought you were a true friend, but I guess money changes people." Tandra raged.

"That's fine if you feel like that, Tandra. I really can't deal with anymore of your drama in my life. If you are using this to define our friendship, then maybe there was really nothing in it to begin with. Anyway, I can't continue to have this banter with you. I'm busy."

Ria slammed her phone back onto the receiver. She refocused her attention back on her computer and channeled her frustration on getting those pages signed off. Her mind kept interrupting and she could not help but ponder on the conversation she had with Tandra. She tapped each of her fingers on her desk to release the frustration she was feeling inside. Even though life was good financially for Ria, issues continued to appear in her life one after the other. Ria put her hand to her head as she tried to stay focused on editing a page.

She sighed at the thought of lending the money to Tandra. She did not want to break their friendship, but she also did not want to be taken for a ride either. Ria had previously paid for Tandra's rent

three times, which made Ria think that Tandra had turned her into the *The Bank of Amer-Ria*. Now she had decided to put her foot down when it came to lending money to her. She had too much to think about now with Shawn, Jackson and the whole deal of parenthood. She now had her son to think about, making sure his future was secure.

*****

Three months had passed since Ria told Shawn about Jackson. Though communication between them had picked up, it still wasn't where Ria wanted it to be. Shawn had called her only twice within the two weeks he had been away. Ria was hesitant on developing the relationship into a stronger friendship. She did not want to fall back in love with Shawn and be left out in the cold.

Ria had decided to hold his visitations with Jackson at Chanel's house, which allowed Ria to supposedly work late so that she would miss running into Shawn and his girlfriend. Ria's view on the whole thing was that she would keep herself out of any baby mama drama and keep her distance. It wasn't about her anymore. As long as Shawn was taking an interest in his son, Ria was satisfied.

Ria flipped through her diary, and above all the important meetings and activities she had jotted down, she looked forward to church on Sunday. She loved the praise and worship at her church. She always came home refreshed and renewed. Yet her emotions still played havoc from time to time. It had been almost two years since she had been with a man, and she was beginning to feel the physical side effects of being alone. She had become so occupied with being a mother and being carried away with her career that she forgot about her heart. A sense of emotional weakness flowed in with the loneliness, which made her feel inadequate in all the things that she put her hands to do. A hug, a kiss, or even a kind compliment was something Ria yearned for.

Ria had thought about getting into a new relationship, but with a demanding toddler and a hectic workload, it seemed too much for her to take on. She knew that there was a lot of closure and healing that needed to be completed in her spirit and soul before she could dive into another relationship. She also had to think about her son, who was now part of the package for a new man to consider. Ria wondered what her life would have been like if she hadn't had Jackson. She deliberately had not spent a lot time with Jackson since she had returned back to LA. The whole mother thing was just something she had a hard time dealing with.

Ria felt trapped. It seemed now that her whole world revolved around her son. She longed for the times when she would just pick herself up and drive to the beach by herself and watch the sun go down. If she wanted to do that now, she would have to organize someone to look after Jackson, pack his bag, make bottles, and the whole nine yards.

Ria opened her desk drawer, searching for her notebook, and her fingers brushed against a little book entitled *Mothers' Daily Devotional*. She remembered receiving it the first time she attended the single-mothers group at church. Ria never gave much thought to read it until now. She picked it up and turned to the day number fourteen, and read it.

Is he worth it? The title caught her attention and she looked more attentively. She almost answered it silently as if it was an actual person questioning her.

Is all your thoughts completely filled with him? Do you know his every thought? What would you do if he was not around?

She was not sure whether to think about Shawn or Jackson on the open questions. Ria was not sure where this was headed, so she read on.

You are probably thinking about a loved one or your children. It's funny how our minds go to everyone else accept Jesus. It is also funny how we also look to those things to bring us healing, joy, and fulfillment. The kind of love that God has for us is called agape love. Have you ever allowed Him to show you that type of love that is fulfilling, brings healing, and gives so much joy?

The words left Ria questioning whether she had truly opened her heart and experienced that agape love. She knew that something had to change as she could not live in this emotional mess, half in-half out type of life. She found herself often dwelling on the past and knew that she had to move on and make a conscious decision about the choices she had made in her life. Ria closed down her computer and got her stuff together. She placed the little devotional book into her bag instead of her desk drawer and headed out to her car.

"See you tomorrow, Clement," Ria said as she passed the security guard, not wanting to stop for conversation.

"Oh, Miss Jackson, how are you? You're sure working late these days."

"I just have a lot of work to do." Ria said.

"A beautiful woman like you should not be working so hard. Your man needs a serious talking to." Ria smiled. "Thanks, Clement, but that is just the way it is". Anyway, have a nice night."

"You, too, Miss Jackson."

Clements's comment lingered with Ria and reinforced the loneliness she felt inside her heart.

As she entered her car and buckled her seat belt, she turned on her CD player, which was playing a Mary Mary album. She had bought a few gospel albums over the past couple months; listening to them seemed to keep her mind at peace from the busy day at work. She often enjoyed the drives home as it was the only time she had to herself alone. As Ria listened to the words to the song, it really began to sink into her heart. Normally, Ria would have caught the words to the song and attempted to sing with it. This time, she remained quiet and allowed the singers to do their job without any interruptions.

Chapter Twenty-Nine

Exhausted, Andréa relaxed herself onto the couch. She had a long day moving her stuff into Shawn's house. Boxes were all over the place, and she wanted to get it sorted out before Shawn got home. Andréa had sold her condo which gave her a tidy profit in her bank account. As she closed her eyes for a small nap, Kenny came down the stairs.

"Hey, miss, how are you doing?"

"I'm tired. I have been back and forth all day, and I still have to move all these boxes before Shawn gets back."

"You want some help?"

"No I should be okay. I just need to get some shut eye for a couple of minutes and then I start back up." Andréa stretched out on the couch and placed herself in a fetal position.

"I'm off to the clinic now.

"All right, see you later," Andréa said with a yawn.

"I'm really happy that you and my brother hooked up. You're the best thing that's happened to him."

"Aww, thanks, Kenny." Andrea said.

"I know it must be difficult, finding out that you're a stepmother and all. Ria will never be half the woman you are." Kenny said.

"That means a lot, knowing the relationship you and Shawn have," Andréa said as she smiled at Kenny.

Before Andréa closed her eyes again, she looked up at the smooth ceiling. She felt like she was in a dream, moving into her dream home with her dream man—life just couldn't get any better.

She pictured what it would be like with her moving around in the house, cooking, living with Shawn day in and day out.

Andréa fantasized about her and Shawn with their own child. Seeing Shawn with Jackson assured Andréa that Shawn was the man she wanted to be the father of her children. She loved seeing him interact with his son. It was a side of him that she had not seen in all the time they had been together. Still Andréa was suspicious to why Ria had not interfered with the parental arrangements or presented any baby mama drama. This somehow intrigued Andréa on the type of person she thought Ria was. She often caught Shawn speaking to her on the phone, and when she asked who he was speaking to, he would say Jonathan or someone else other than Ria. Andréa knew that she had to do her own undercover investigations to find out what Ria was up to.

Andréa was introduced to Tandra at a networking event and found out she was looking for an investor for her hair salon/training center. She initially was not that interested until Tandra invited her to her home. There, she saw a picture of Tandra and Ria on the mantel piece. Andréa had informed Tandra that she was with Shawn, highlighting a conflict of interest. But as Tandra continued to confide in Andréa about Ria not helping her out monetarily, she also spoke extensively about why Shawn and Ria broke up. Andrea concluded that this was a good investment not just for business but for pleasure. Every now and then, a small pinch of doubt would rise up in her soul, making her think that she was making a mistake. Andréa pushed it away and diagnosed her trust issues to her past experience in relationships.

Andréa dozed off in a peaceful sleep, until her cell phone awoke her. She groaned and picked it up from inside her handbag.

"Hello, Andréa speaking."

"Good afternoon, Andréa. It's Pastor Michael."

"Oh, hi Pastor Mike." Andréa fixed herself in a seating position.

"I thought I'd call you. It's been a long time since I've seen you at church, and my wife and I were concerned."

"Well, I have been so busy at work and all…it's been a bit

difficult to come."

"Okay, so how is life treating you?" Pastor Mike said.

Andréa began to feel awkward and transparent. She had been thinking about calling her pastor, but the guilt of her and Shawn being intimate with each other made it very difficult for her to speak to her pastor. "Well…good. I'm just getting on with it."

"Hmm, so how is the relationship going?"

"Relationship?" Andréa said with a nervous laugh. "How did you know I was in a relationship?"

"God has a funny way of revealing things."

"Well, I was going to call you and let you know the good news. I'm getting engaged."

"Are you sure that you're ready for that?" He said diffusing her excitement.

This was not the response Andréa was expecting. She hesitated. "What do you mean by that, Pastor Mike?"

"Is he the right man for you, and is he in line with what God has destined for you?"

"I believe he is. I've not been this happy in a long time, Pastor Mike. He just needs a little encouragement in coming to church, and I believe he is a God-fearing man. And half of the time, he's in another state, so it's hard for him. He's been going through such a hard time lately and…"

"It's okay, Andréa. You really don't need to convince me. I tell you what, why don't both of you come down to the church office on Wednesday night, about eight. We can at least arrange a pre-marital meeting. How does that sound?"

"Pre-marital classes? We haven't even set a date yet." Andréa rolled her eyes, irritated and bothered by her pastor's call. "Pastor Michael, to be honest with you, I don't think that would be necessary. I don't think we need it. We are both adults not teenagers"

Andréa knew how counseling sessions worked, and she knew Shawn would not be up to revealing things in their relationship that he considered private. Andréa also did not want to rock the boat with them, especially with Ria hovering around him.

"We know what to expect in marriage, and Shawn also has a very hectic schedule. Most weekends, he visits his son. I'm also very busy with work," Andréa said sharply.

"He has a son?"

"Yes, Pastor, from a previous relationship," Andréa said.

"Are you ready to take on all of that? Blended families are a lot of hard work."

Andréa sighed loudly. "Don't you think I have considered that, Pastor? I'm not a child."

"I know that. I am just concerned. Anyway, even if your partner can't come, I would still like to see you."

"All right, Pastor, I'll try," Andréa said in order to end the conversation.

After Andréa closed her cell phone, she felt more irritated than she'd ever felt before while talking to her Pastor. Andréa exhaled and lay back onto the couch. She had to admit she felt bad for being disrespectful to her pastor and wondered if she should call him to apologize. Even now, that tugging feeling that she had felt before was even stronger, and it burdened her. It also brought to the surface her spiritual relationship that she had neglected. How quickly her dream bubble had burst, and the reality of what she had compromised appeared. Andréa stood from her seated position, the nap she once craved overthrown by her troubled conscience.

*****

Shawn sat on the hotel bed while he closed his suitcase. He walked into the luxurious hotel bathroom for one last quick inspection to see if there were any other items he had forgotten to pack. Shawn took his cell phone out of his back pocket and began to dial. As it rang, Shawn took a seat by the huge window and viewed the San Diego skyline from the eighth floor. He was welcomed by Ria's voicemail.

"Ria, it's me, Shawn. When you get this message, if you can give me a call, it would be very much appreciated." Shawn was disappointed. He really wanted to talk to Ria and see how his son was doing. He missed them. Shawn continued to stand by the window, looking at the skyline reflecting on life. He really missed his mom at times like this. He wanted to ask her approval of whether he was being a good dad. Whether he was making the right choice of getting engaged to a woman he was not sure he loved. The closeness Ria had with his mother made it hard for him to disconnect with her. Deep down his heart still belong with her, which made loving Andréa harder.

Chapter Thirty

ia had just entered her office from a three-hour corporate meeting. She was so desperate for coffee that she was willing to chew on some coffee beans. As she reached her desk, she noticed three missed calls on her cell phone, including one voice message.

"Candy, can you make me some coffee, please?" she asked.

"No problem, Miss Jackson. I'll have it on your desk within five minutes."

"Thank you."

Ria sat on her leather chair and viewed the list of missed calls. One was from her mother, and Ria rolled her eyes. The other two were from Shawn and Tandra. It came as a bit of surprise that Tandra had called her. It had been a couple of months since she had spoken to her. Ria's personal assistant came in with her coffee. Ria whispered her thanks with a smile.

After she listened to Shawn's message, she deleted it and noticed that the tone of his voice was not as confident as she knew him to sound. Ria decided to call him back. She knew that he had gone to San Diego, but was not sure what time he was coming back. As she heard his phone ringing, Ria became a bit anxious on what he wanted to talk to her about. Instead of him answering, she got his voicemail, so she left a message.

"Hi Shawn, it's Ri. I got your message. I hope you're all right. Just want to let you know that I'm here if you need me."

It was four o'clock and Ria decided to do something different—she decided to leave the office early and go to the beach. She just wanted time alone and away from being a mother.

She did not want to go to her sister's and be hassled by her son, neither did she want to go home and look at the things that needed to be done around the house. She wanted her own peaceful breathing space.

Before packing up, she decided to call Tandra. In the event of Tandra giving her a round-two of the conversation they'd had a couple of months ago, she thought it best to contact her before she went to the beach and reclaimed her peace. Ria picked up her cell and balanced it between her ear and shoulder.

"Hi Tandra, I got your missed call." Ria said.

"Hey, Ria, how are you? It's been a long time girl."

"It sure has. How are you?" Ria said.

"I'm doing real good." Tandra said.

"How is the business venture going?" Ria did not want to ask, but she felt obligated to.

"It's going good. I managed to get a partner and things are going well. In fact, I had the opening night for the salon last week."

"Oh, that's good!" Despite their friendship cracking, Ria was hurt she hadn't been invited. "Wow, that was quick. I am really happy for you. So who is this new business partner then?" Ria said teasingly, insinuating that it was a man.

"Well, I met *her* at a networking event. She is a personal chef to celebrities, and when I told her about my vision, she was extremely enthusiastic about it. She really is a strong believer in giving back to the community. We have become really good friends over the past couple of months."

Ria sensed the sarcasm coming from Tandra's tone. She ignored it. "I can still recommend you to sponsors, if you like."

"Oh no, that is fine, girl. We have two major sponsors already. She's well connected in the industry."

"It sounds like you have everything sorted out. I'm excited for you. How are the kids?" Ria tried her best to sound genuinely happy for Tandra even though she felt guilty for not supporting her.

"Oh, they're fine. You know how troublesome they can be. How's Jackson?"

"Getting bigger and more demanding. But he's pretty good apart from that. It's his first birthday next week. I can't believe he's going to be one already."

"Yep, time flies when you're raising children." Ria said.

"Why don't you and your business partner come down to Chanel's house for Jackson's birthday?"

Tandra hesitated before answering. "I'll check with her, but that sounds like a good idea. So…Ria, how are things with you and Shawn?" Ria was slightly taken aback from the quick diversion of conversation topic. "It seems to be going all right. I mean, he's taking good care of his son and seeing him every chance he can get."

"But what about you and him? Do you want him back? You know he's with someone else now." Tandra said fishing.

Ria did not trust nor appreciate the sharp tone Tandra was using. It made her feel like Tandra was up to something.

"I'm very much aware that he's with someone, Tandra. You, of all people, should know that. I choose to stay out of his personal business. As long as he's looking after his son, I am satisfied."

Tandra caught on to Ria's defensive response, so she decided to change her method. "I think you're dealing with the whole situation very well."

"Anyway, Tandra, I was just about to step out the office."

"Email me the details for Jackson's party, and I will try to be there."

"I'll do that in about an hour." Ria said.

Chapter Thirty-One

*D*aniel looked around the huge office and began to bob his head to the music playing in the background. Traci looked at him and gave him a disappointed look as if he were a child. "Can't you be serious for one minute?"

"I'm just enjoying the music. I like Kirk Franklin. You don't like him?"

Traci looked at Daniel again and before she could even respond, she was interrupted by the entrance of a short white guy. The man took a seat opposite them, and he glanced at them and offered a friendly smile.

"How y'all doing?" This was their fourth marriage counseling session. "You folks beginning to fast and pray together now?"

Traci nodded while Daniel was still trying to work out how a white pastor was able to run a predominantly black church.

"How are things going with you, Brother Daniel? I see you're back at work." The pastor grinned at Daniel.

"Yeah, I'm really happy about that. Generally, things are getting better between us. I think now we are beginning to have a better understanding of each other." Daniel looked at Traci, waiting for her agreement. Traci nodded.

Things had started to slowly improve between them since they had been attending church and marriage counseling.

"You see, marriage is like the seasons. You see, there are winter, fall, spring, and summer." The pastor paused before he continued. "Y'all been married a long time now and need to recognize the different seasons or phases your marriage goes through. You also need to prepare for each season. Right now, you may be experiencing a winter season, which means you have to keep covered because the elements, atmosphere around you, can make you sick."

Daniel nodded.

"How do you keep covered, you may ask, when your marriage is going through a winter season? You keep it covered in the word of God, the blood of Jesus, and out of the reach of people."

Daniel continued to nod as Traci listened.

Since Daniel had been attending church with Traci, his desire for the fast life slowly diminished. However, he wasn't sure if the change had to do with him not being popular or with him really wanting to make a go at his marriage.

"So how did you find it?" Traci asked as they walked outside the church chapel into the warm air.

"Very interesting," Daniel said as he smiled.

"What do you mean by interesting?"

"He made a lot of sense. I like what he said about a woman being a man's rib and the seasons of marriage. I remember when I first saw you. I knew you would be my wife. There was just something inside of telling me you were the one."

Traci was so surprised by how Daniel, had taken to her pastor and the whole going back to church thing. It was the first time in years Daniel had spoken about the past and the feelings he had for her. Over the couple of months, while she continued to pray and fast for her marriage, she could see the sincerity of Daniel's love coming back into his eyes. It had not been easy,

she still carried a lot of distrust in her heart. Many nights she cried herself to sleep when Daniel was playing away from home. Traci was still tormented by the possibility of Daniel still playing around with men. It plagued her mind like a disease. Because of this, they still had not restored the intimate part of their marriage.

"How was it for you, honey?" Daniel said while he opened Traci's car door and waited for her to be seated before closing it.

"I'm learning a lot, but we still got a long way to go."

"I know, but the most important thing is that we're on the same page, right, working together?" Daniel said as they drove home.

Chapter Thirty-Two

*A*s Ria kicked her front door shut, the escalating cry of her son filled every corner of her large apartment. She walked into the sitting room and placed him in his playpen. This seemed to annoy Jackson even more. He now could stand up without support. He held on to the side of his playpen and stood, declaring war with his mother. Ria ignored him and walked over to the kitchen to fix his dinner.

"You're gonna have to keep crying until I fix your food," Ria said sternly.

Ria was relieved that she was able to spend at least half an hour at the beach. It helped her regain the peace that she needed to keep calm in the midst of a demanding screaming toddler. She still had not heard from Shawn, but she would give him time to call her back before she started worrying. As she placed a small plate of mashed potatoes and chicken in the microwave, she managed to hear her doorbell buzzer over the sound of her screaming son. Ria strolled down her hallway in her pumps and work attire, and straightened her posture in the event of a guest being at her door. As she opened her front door, the sound of her son's cry bellowed out from the door. To her surprise, Shawn was standing in front of her. She looked at him with a frown, still trying to take in the fact that he was actually standing at her door.

"Hey Mama," Shawn said as he bent down and kissed her cheek.

"Oh my god, I was just thinking of you. But I wasn't expecting you to turn up on my door step." She stood there, still looking at him.

While she inspected him from head to toe, he looked questionably at her, and then over her shoulder in response to his crying son.

"So are you going to invite me in so I can see what's wrong with my son?"

"yeah, sorry. Come in. The place is a bit of a mess—I just stepped in myself. Don't mind your mini-me over there. He just needs some food."

As Shawn walked passed her, she noticed he looked just how she liked him to look. Even though they communicated regularly on the phone, it had been quite a while since they had seen each other.

"Nice place, very nice," Shawn said as he walked through the broad white hallway.

"Did you just fly in from San Diego?"

Shawn walked straight toward his screaming child and picked him up. "Yeah, I thought I'd pay you guys a visit. I got your message."

As Jackson was lifted up into his father's arms, his bellowing cry calmed down to a small moan. Ria walked over to the microwave while Shawn took a seat on the sofa and placed Jackson on his lap. Shawn glanced around the huge room and smiled. "This apartment is very you."

"I take that as a compliment," Ria said as she took Jackson from Shawn's arms and placed him in his high chair. Jackson's cry elevated again, and Ria tried unsuccessfully to disguise her frustration.

"It's all right. I'll feed him here," Shawn offered.

"Let me warn you first of my carpet, and secondly that you better have an extra shirt because he's going to mess up the one you have on."

Ria returned to the kitchen in her pumps, trying not to sway her hips. She knew Shawn was watching her walk off. Ria brought Jackson's small plate of warmed food and a spoon into the sitting area. Shawn took the plate of food and began to feed Jackson, who was eagerly awaiting his meal with his slobbery mouth wide open.

From the kitchen, Ria called out, "You hungry, Shawn? You want some food?"

"Yeah, bring it on."

Ria smiled as she busied herself in her the kitchen. She glanced back at Shawn and Jackson. She was glad that things were turning out better between them both. She was now able to appreciate Shawn as just the father of her child, and not her ex. Her pastor once said to her, "Time is a great healer." Ria could now understand his statement. It seemed that something else had taken the place of that yearning, that pining she once had for Shawn.

"How's your girlfriend?" Ria asked while keeping her back toward him. She paused, waiting for his answer.

Shawn did a fake cough as if he had something stuck in his throat.

"Who, Andréa?"

"You have more than one girlfriend now?" Ria teased. She knew that he found it difficult talking about his girlfriend with her.

"She's all right, she's good."

"Somehow, she looks familiar, but I can't quite place her." Ria waited for his response.

"It's college. She was in my business class," Shawn said reluctantly.

"Oh yeah, that's right." Ria walked back over to where Shawn and Jackson were sitting. She bent over and reached for her stereo remote control, which was on the table nearest Shawn. "So how's your relationship going?" Ria looked straight into Shawn's eyes with a teasing smile.

Shawn tried not to be hypnotized by Ria's game, but found it difficult to concentrate. He stuttered as he tried to find a response. "We…We're just trying to make it work, that's all."

"That's good. I'm happy for you both," Ria said with a genuine smile. She leaned toward the stereo. "You don't mind, do you, if I play a little music? I'm just going to slip into something more comfortable before I get Jackson ready for bed."

As Ria left Shawn in the living room, she entered into her

bedroom. Shawn continued to feed Jackson, who was now refusing to eat. "You don't want to take one more spoonful?"

Shawn placed the spoon in front of Jackson's mouth, but Jackson shook his head and pushed the plate away from his face, unexpectedly knocking it out of Shawn's hands onto the carpet. Shawn looked in horror as mashed potatoes and chicken splattered onto the forbidden carpet. Jackson, seeing the expression on his father's face, began to giggle. Shawn could not help but laugh at his son's amusement.

"Oh boy, your mamma gonna kill me."

Jackson continued to giggle. Shawn quickly placed Jackson into his playpen, who decided to settle down and entertain himself with the toys he had in there. Shawn walked over to the kitchen and saw paper towels on a chrome holder. He grabbed a few sheets and observed the kitchen, which was well organized, clean and inviting. Shawn already felt comfortable and at home. Everything, even though in a different house, was still familiar to him. The toaster, the tea and coffee arrangement was placed in the same position as they'd had it when they were living together. Just as Shawn turned around, Ria crept up behind him, startling him slightly.

"What you doing in my kitchen with tissue in your hand?" Ria asked playfully.

"Jackson had a little accident with his food."

"On my beautiful cream carpet? Give me that tissue." Ria teased.

"It's okay, I got it."

"You should have got it before it fell on my carpet," Ria said humorously as she walked toward the microwave and placed a plate of rice and stew chicken in it. "You can turn on the TV and turn off the music if you want. The remote is on the table," Ria shouted from the kitchen.

"Nah, that's all right. The music's good. Just make sure I get a good portion of stew chicken."

The aroma of food filled the room, it was nostalgic for Shawn. He missed Ria's home cooking. Even though Andréa could cook

her butt off, there was just something missing. As Shawn managed to wipe up Jackson's mess, Ria came over with a silver tray and a blue napkin in her hand. Shawn grinned like a child receiving a present on Christmas. He got up from his knees and took the tray from Ria with one hand while Ria took the tissue from him.

"Is that portion all right? Wasn't sure of…"

"No, honey, that's fine."

Ria felt a little butterfly in her stomach at the sound of Shawn calling her *honey*. She was not expecting a simple term of endearment to pull that type of emotion. Still, she did not want Shawn to realize that she was moved by his affectionate name-calling. She strode back into the kitchen and tried to brush it off by singing to her Vivian Green CD, which was playing in the background. While Jackson continued to play happily in his play pen, Shawn ate his food like a man who had not eaten for two days. Ria entered the room with a smaller plate of food, and sat almost opposite to Shawn on the left-hand side of the sofa.

"You hungry, huh?" she mocked.

"Good food." Shawn said he looked at Ria with a glance that brought those butterflies flying stronger in her stomach.

Ria cleared her throat and broke the glance that she almost got caught in. She returned her attention to her stew chicken.

*****

The conversation flowed between them until it was late in the evening. The curtains had been drawn and the room was lit lightly with two side lamps reflecting Ria's and Shawn's shadows upon the side of the wall. The table before them had two glasses of half drunken wine with an empty wine bottle.

Ria leaped from her seated position. "Oh my goodness, do you remember this song back in college? It was the bomb, not like this crap they have now. *She's playing hard to get…*" Ria began to sing in tune with the song. Shawn watched and admired Ria as she moved across the room.

"Didn't I buy this track for you?" Shawn asked.

"Yes, you did. I think in '93." Ria stretched out her hand toward Shawn, playfully inviting him to join her.

Shawn rolled his eyes and held on to Ria's hand, reluctantly joining her. "You know fast songs aren't really my thing."

"Oh come on, we're just having some fun. I promise if the next song is slow, I'll slow dance with you."

The next song was slow, encouraging them to draw closer to each other. Shawn placed his hand softly upon Ria's waist. They looked into each other's eyes. This time, Ria was hooked. Ria automatically positioned her arms around Shawn's broad shoulders, resting her hands upon his neck. The atmosphere grew into a sentimental mood from the sociable mood they had attained throughout the evening. The barriers that Ria once had grew weak, and she could feel herself melting in his arms.

Shawn began to sing the words to the song, overlapping Keith Washington's smooth vocals. That was it. Ria was now open and defenseless—her heart, emotions, her conviction was completely lost. As the song continued, Ria looked deeply into Shawn's face, examining every detail. Ria missed this part of love. She almost forgot how good it felt to be romanced and in Shawn's arms again. She bit the side of her lip, anticipating the next move. Shawn moved his face closer. What once felt so awkward now felt too natural.

Their lips touched, Ria did not pull away. It felt so right for her to be in his arms again. They continued to embrace each other in a kiss. They both knew that they were still tied in a love that they thought had been cut.

Chapter Thirty-Three

*A*ndréa awoke from her bedroom, she was startled by a huge thump. She got up from the bed, rubbing her neck from the bad sleeping position she was in. As she investigated the sound, she heard the loud bang again. She headed to where the noises were coming from.

"Shawn, is that you?" Andréa called out. The thumping and noise increased as Andréa moved toward the stairwell and ascended the steps. "Shawn, Shawn." Andréa called his name in a stern, yet concerned tone. As she reached the top of the stairs, she became aware of where the noise was coming from, and who the guilty culprit was. Andréa walked toward Kenny's bedroom door.

"Kenny, are you all right in there?" Andréa looked at her watch. It was 10:30 in the morning. Where was Shawn? Andréa reluctantly knocked on Kenny's door again as the noise continued. "Hey, Kenny, what's going on in there?"

"Leave me alone, Andréa." There was another noise, like glass shattering.

"Oh my God, what's going on?"

"I told you, woman, leave me alone."

Stricken with concern, Andréa turned the handle and opened Kenny's door. She was stunned by the view before her. The King-sized bed that stood in the middle of his room was turned on its side. The side table and everything that was in the room had been removed from its original place. As her eyes searched the room, she saw a trail of thick red blood on the light blue carpet. She followed it to the en-suite bathroom. She walked in and screamed.

There Kenny stood with a belt wrapped around his arm, with blood oozing out from different pin points of his arm.

"What did I tell you?" Kenny shouted.

"Kenny, you need help…"

"Shut up and get out. I'm warning you." Kenny threatened.

"Please, Kenny, you don't need to do this." As Andréa tried to step closer, Kenny drew out the needle that was plunged into his arm and charged toward Andréa with it. Her hazel eyes widened and she stepped backwards slowly, but the more she stepped back, the closer and quicker Kenny came. She turned to run, but could feel Kenny's footsteps right behind her. Andréa's heart beat so hard that she could feel it banging against her rib cage. Fear blurred her vision, but she managed to stay focused enough to run into the guest room and slam the door closed, locking it. Kenny hit the closed door. Breathless and full of panic, Andréa placed her hand on her chest, her body shaking as if she was having an epileptic fit.

Tears of fear streamed down her face as she slid to the floor and stayed. She was in two minds whether to call the police. On one hand, she didn't want to get Kenny in trouble. But she didn't want to die either. As she attempted to calm herself, she heard Kenny run downstairs and slam the front door. Andréa took three deep breaths in, and then exhaled out slowly. She located the phone with her red eyes and crawled over to it. She dialed Shawn's number and waited for it to ring.

*****

Shawn's cell phone rang, and he glanced at it on his dashboard. He saw Andréa's number and decided to ignore it. He did not want to explain to Andréa where he had spent the night. He was scared of what might happen if they had an argument. He knew the way he was feeling about Ria could jeopardize their engagement. He did not want to put Andréa through another heartache by ending their relationship. Being with Ria and his son was everything he had dreamed about. But something about Ria had changed, and he felt less confident that she would take him back if he left Andréa. He wasn't sure whether her distance was due to him being in a relationship, or because she had someone else. All he knew was that he was still deeply in love with her. Watching the woman he always loved mother his child was an emotional experience.

As Shawn drove into his garage, he wondered what he would tell Andréa. He sat in the car for a minute before he got out and entered his house from the garage. He took his travel bag from the trunk of his car. He was happy that he left his car at his friend Jonathan's house. It would have been an awkward situation if Ria had dropped him home.

Inside the hallway, Shawn loosened his trainers, then walked upstairs with his traveling bag. He noticed that the house was peculiarly quiet. His cell phone rang from downstairs as he called out Andréa's name. He ignored the phone and continued climbing the steps. When Shawn reached the top of the stairs, Andréa slowly emerged from the guest room, her limbs shaking like a leaf in a winter storm.

"What's wrong, Andréa?"

Andréa ran toward Shawn and held him so tight that he could feel her heart beat against his chest. "Who did this to you?" Shawn asked protectively. "Did someone break into the house? Who was it?"

Andréa cried and shook her head. "N—no—" She tried to talk through the shaking, but it was hard for Shawn to understand what she was saying. "I—I don't know what happened. Kenny had a needle in his arm, and he st—started to chase me. I ran and hid, I—I tried to call you, b—but I couldn't get you."

"Oh baby, I can't believe Kenny. I'm so sorry. I shouldn't have left you alone with him. I was stupid."

Shawn held Andréa in his arms until her shaking calmed. They walked to the bedroom and Shawn sat Andréa down. As she sat on the bed, he crouched down before her and looked into her hazel eyes. "Look, I'm sorry. I shouldn't have exposed you to that."

"I was so scared. I thought he was going to kill me. He needs

help, serious help, Shawn." Andrea said.

"I just don't know what to do. I've tried to give him the best. Chances after chances but..." Shawn said.

"You have done all that you can do. We're trying to build a life now, and a family." Andrea said more calmly.

Andréa was fond of Kenny, but after what he had done to her, she didn't want him nowhere near her. She felt like she had taken on so much with Shawn, and the burden of it was stressing her out. Andréa, being of a strong mind, still convinced herself that he was meant for her. She once again pushed aside her anxieties and decided that she would focus on not failing at another relationship. It was times like this that she missed going to church and having that faith that she knew would pull her through such a situation. Andréa loved Shawn to pieces. Aside from him having a child, the mood swings, and dealing with a drug addict brother, he was everything she had needed in a man. So she thought.

"You know what?" Andréa said, her voice calm. "I have such a full day today, I better get on with it."

"You sure you gonna be okay to work?"

"I'll be fine. The whole thing just shook me up a little. You are here now."

Andréa managed to pull off a smile for him. He had a way of making her feel like that young girl back in college, weak and mesmerized by his charm.

As Andréa went into the bathroom, she remembered the promises she had made and broken to God. It plagued her that she was living in sin. What if Kenny had killed her? Being in a life-threatening situation made her wonder if she was on the right path that God had designed for her.

After applying her face scrub and rinsing it off, she stared at her reflection in the mirror. "We need to set a date, Shawn," Andréa shouted from the bathroom.

"A date for what?"

"Our wedding."

"Oh yeah…we'll set a date. But there's no rush, is there?"

"What do you mean, there's no rush? What's stopping us?"

Andrea said.

"Nothing. I was just waiting on you. I know it's a big thing for women. All I need to do is show up, right?"

Andréa looked over her shoulder at Shawn and glared at him. After the Kenny incident, she was hoping for a better response than what Shawn had given. But she remained calm. Once she was married to the man of her dreams, she hoped things would get better. Andréa shuddered off the thought of being single again. She returned to the bedroom while drying her face on a thick white towel.

"Baby, I don't need anything big. Why don't we just elope, just me and you and a couple of people, close friends?"

"Sounds—good. Where did you have in mind?" Shawn asked while unpacking his clothes from his travel bag.

"I was thinking Hawaii or the Bahamas."

"It sounds good. Why don't you look into it and let me know?"

Shawn was not as enthusiastic as Andréa wanted him to be. "Anyway, don't you have your business luncheon this week?"

"Yes, I do. I still have some loose ends to tie up.," Andréa said.

"Don't you want to concentrate on that first? You know I've got to get Kenny sorted out. I'm not sure if it's the right time."

"What do you mean?" Andréa asked hopelessly. "We spoke about this before. I can't keep holding out. I've sacrificed a lot for you. Doesn't that mean anything to you at all?"

All Andréa knew was that she was marrying Shawn come hell or high water. What she had sacrificed to have him had to count for something.

"I see all the sacrifices you've made, and I know that any other woman would have run a mile by now. But I have a lot of things to consider now. I'm sorry that I've come with all this baggage, but this is me." Shawn stated.

Shawn walked closer to Andréa and held her waist. She tried to pull away.

"We need to set a date. Otherwise, I'm moving out."

Andréa wanted to call Shawn's bluff. What she had started to

learn about Shawn was that he was needy and hated to be alone. If his brother had been around, she knew she wouldn't have stood a chance.

"What time span were you thinking of?" Shawn asked with reluctance.

"Twelve weeks' time. I know it's around the corner, but we can just have a quiet and private ceremony and do something bigger at a later date."

Shawn frowned.

"Look, I know you're concerned about Kenny, but we will deal with it together, okay?"

Shawn found it hard to turn down the deal. Right now, with Ria, Jackson, and his career on one hand and Kenny on the other, it was too much to carry by himself.

Chapter Thirty-Four

"You going to that party tonight, Danny boy?"

"Naw, man, it's not my scene anymore."

"Oh come on, it's gonna be fun. It's just a celebration party."

Both Daniel and his teammate Lance were in the locker room getting dressed to go home. They had played a home game, and the Stallions had won.

"I'm trying to start a family and come away from all the parties." Daniel said.

"It's just a celebration party, with a lot of industry people attending."

Even though Daniel was back playing for the Stallions, he was not making the money he used to since the knife injury. The injury had left him with a less than perfect performance.

"I really could use some extra cash right now. It's hard maintaining my lifestyle on a small salary, man," Daniel said

"You should have told me. I got a friend that's coming. I'll introduce you to him. He'll hook you up with the best sponsor going." Lance said.

"Naw, I don't know. I told you I'm trying to stay away from that now. I'm not trying to party like I use to."

"That don't mean nothin'. I've got two kids and one on the way. I even go to church every Sunday and pay my tithes. Just for that sponsor alone, you need to come, even if it's for an hour."

Daniel thought for a couple of seconds while Lance closed his locker and hooked his bag over his shoulder.

"So you coming then?" Lance asked.

"Yeah, I'll come with my wife."

Lanced stopped and looked at Daniel as to ask why. "Okay, *family man*, you come with your wife. I'll text you the details."

The prospect of getting a sponsor excited Daniel. He was sick and tired of watching every penny that came in and out. Daniel missed his old lifestyle. The respect he had gained was something he wished he had back. Daniel locked his locker, said goodbye to the rest of his teammates, and walked outside toward his car. He was looking forward to his home-cooked meal when he got home.

*****

Daniel kept his eyes firmly on the road as he drove home; his mind replayed the conversation he'd just had with Lance. He knew Lance was still living the DL lifestyle, but it surprised him that his wife had not noticed the dangerous game he was playing. He envied Lance. The man had it all, and it didn't cost him anything. He had all the money, excellent athletic ability, a wife, children, and the lifestyle someone would kill to have. Not only did Michael live the lifestyle, but he went to church and paid his tithes. He was living a blessed life, and here Daniel was struggling. If Lance could have the best of both worlds, why couldn't he?

With his growling belly motivating him to drive faster, Daniel swiftly parked his car, entered his home, and followed the sweet aroma of roast pork to the kitchen. As he approached the counter top, he saw a note Traci had left, informing him that she was spending the night at her sister's house and his plate of food was in the microwave. Daniel crumpled the note and set the microwave. His cell phone began to vibrate, and he took it from his back pocket. It was a text message with the address details to the party. He decided to call Traci straight away and inform her of his evening plans.

*****

After Ria dropped Jackson off at the church day care facility, she relaxed. Jackson had kept her up all night. It was one of the things she started to notice with Jackson. Every time he spent time with Shawn, he would give her a hard time the night after. Another thing that weighed heavily on her heart was the night she'd spent with Shawn. They had come close to being intimate, but Ria stopped him just in time. She was fed up with the roller coaster ride she was going through with Shawn, and she wanted to be free.

She walked into the main hall of the church, in search of her friend Clara. She had found a good friend in Clara. Even though Ria was reluctant to reveal all her business to her, she was happy to find a listening ear. She enjoyed the non-judgmental, understanding advice that Clara freely gave. Just like Ria, Clara was also a single mother leading a successful career, and it seemed that they had a lot in common.

"Hey Clara, I thought I was going to be late," Ria said as she slid across the pew toward Clara.

"No, no, you're still on time. The praise and worship team aren't even on stage yet. Are you okay?"

"I'm just a little tired. Jackson kept me up all night," Ria said with a yawn.

"You've done well to make it. I would have stayed home and caught up on some sleep."

"It was a case of either going crazy at home or coming out to reclaim my sanity." They chuckled.

Ria closed her eyes to say a private prayer. Lord, please could you strengthen me? I no longer want to live a life of chaos. Please let me know that you are there for me and free me from all these crazy emotions.

As the praise and worship team approached the stage and began to sing "God Is Here," Ria felt a whole peace come over. It was as if someone had touched her softly on her head. She turned around in case it was someone she knew. But when she glanced behind her, she failed to recognize any of the people. Ria stood with the rest of the congregation and started to sing. Each word was projected out of her soul. She started singing with so much

passion she could not control herself. Tears trickled down her cheeks, and she found herself bending down to her knees. Ria did not care who was watching her. She poured out the contents of her soul and with each word, she felt more and more liberated.

Ria was not sure how long she was on her knees, but in the midst of her experience, she heard Pastor Joseph call her name. Two male ushers came to help her to the front. She still found it hard to stand.

"You can leave her there now," Pastor Joseph said calmly.

Ria sunk to her knees again, this time in front of the church. Pastor Joseph walked up to Ria with a smile and held the microphone to Ria's mouth. The sound that came out of her spirit caused members of the congregation to join her on her knees in worship. Ria slowly got off her knees and faced the congregation. As she sang, she could not quite comprehend the beautiful vocals of her voice and accepted that it must be one of the worship leaders singing along with her. Her eyes skimmed through the congregation, and she saw Chanel on her knees with her arms up high. Ria felt so light and refreshed. The tiredness had evaporated, and it felt like her strength had been restored.

Breathing heavily, she handed the microphone over to Pastor Joseph. He put his arm on her shoulder and stood in front of her. The instruments played softly in the background, allowing the congregation to settle down. Ria held her chest.

"That was you singing, you do know that, don't you?" Ria stared at him in disbelief. "You know that this has been a long time coming. Jesus is now waiting for you with open arms, and He is calling you. Will you accept Him into your life to reign and rule?"

"Yes," Ria said with tears in her eyes. "I repent for all my sins because I cannot do this thing by myself."

Applause and shouts of praise flowed through the atmosphere. Chanel ran over to Ria and hugged her with tears in her eyes.

Chapter Thirty-Five

*D*aniel poured two glasses of Bacardi from his mini bar. The sitting room was dimly lit. It was not by Daniel's choice that Lance's friend Tyler would be in his home. But that was the way things had turned out, and Daniel was fighting it. After pondering on how Lance was living, he was becoming more convinced that he could have it both ways and still be blessed.

It had been such a long time since Daniel conversed in this type of company. Even though his intuition told him to stop and flee, he decided to fight it and walk into a place which was all too familiar to him.

"Don't worry. I'll sort you out a nice tasty contract," Tyler said as he gave Daniel an intense look with his green eyes.

"I would really appreciate that, Ty," Daniel said slowly. They had gotten so comfortable with each other in such a short period of time; their mutual attraction was increasingly evident.

"Anyway, I got to go." Tyler said.

"Oh?" Daniel said, surprised by Tyler's quick departure.

"I'm flying out to Las Vegas tomorrow, so I better get back home to pack. I'll invite you down to my pad when I get back."

"That would be great. I love it up there." Daniel said.

"Yeah, it's pretty cool. We'll be able to discuss things in *more* detail."

There was more to what Tyler was saying, but Daniel preferred to keep his response platonic. As he saw Tyler out to his car, he had a sense of concern on where this would lead to. The excitement that he once would have felt was absent. Having to jeopardize all that he had built up with Traci to go back to sneaking around did not seem worth it.

*****

Tandra was bored out of her mind while sitting in the bridal boutique. She wondered how long she would be able to keep this façade up before Andréa noticed. As Andrea stepped out behind the changing room curtains, Tandra once again put her falsity to the test.

"Oh Andréa, you look so beautiful in that dress. I can't believe you'll be getting married soon," she said with a phony tone unrecognizable to Andréa.

Andréa step onto a white cushioned pedestal of Beautiful Brides boutique. "You really like it? I didn't want to have a big cathedral-style dress as we'll be on the beach. It would've been too heavy."

"No, girl, it's perfect."

Andréa looked at her reflection in the mirror and admired herself. Indeed she knew that she made a beautiful bride, but it still did not feel natural to her. She had tried on almost fifty dresses in fourteen different bridal shops, but she could not shake off the feeling that she was making a mistake. "I do look good in this, don't I? The diamonds complement my hazel eyes, don't you think?"

The shop assistant nodded in agreement with a predictable smile.

"I'll take it," Andréa said as she walked back into the dressing room. As Tandra looked at her own reflection, she rolled her eyes and looked at her watch. *I was wondering when this heifer was going to finish*, she muttered under her breath while fixing her hair.

Andréa walked out with a bounce in her step and gave Tandra a smile. "Thanks for being there. You're a good friend. I was thinking, do you want to get something to eat? My treat?"

"Well it would have to be a quick snack. I left the kids with my aunt, and she really gets an attitude when I leave them later than

expected," Tandra lied.

"We can go to a cute little bistro a few blocks from here or a tapas restaurant, your choice. I'll drop you off at your aunt's house afterwards."

"Tapas? Ooh, child, I love me some tapas. My aunt can wait. I'll deal with her stank attitude when I get there." After Andréa had paid for her wedding dress, they both exited the beautiful boutique.

The day was bright and the atmosphere was just right. Ria loved the freedom she now felt. She could finally look at Jackson without seeing Shawn. It was now, looking from the outside in, that she realized how much of herself was tied in Shawn. Ria was happy that all emotional ties were now broken from her mind, body, and soul. She had a new man in her life called Jesus.

Jackson threw one of his stuffed animal toys out of his pushchair, and Ria bent down to pick it up. As she got up, she happened to see Tandra and Andréa walking in her direction. Ria was puzzled. It was too late to walk back or dive into a shop. She decided to walk confidently toward them.

Tandra noticed Ria, and she looked both stunned and embarrassed.

"Ria, girl, what a coincidence. You are looking so good," Tandra prattled on. "Look at my little man, isn't he getting big?" Tandra said.

"It is a coincidence seeing both of you here. How are you both?" Ria said in a cool and mellow tone. She could see that Andréa was trying to ignore her by pretending to look into a window of a shop.

"Well, I'm sure Shawn has told you," Andréa said as she reluctantly faced Ria. Confused, Ria looked at Tandra for a clue. Tandra bent down to play with Jackson in order to keep herself out of an awkward situation.

"Shawn and I are getting married in six weeks. In fact, Tandra helped me choose my dress today," Andréa said pompously.

"Well, congratulations! I'm pleased for both of you," Ria said diplomatically as Tandra looked at Ria as if she had not heard right. "If it's only six weeks away, you must have a lot of work to do."

"Well, with good friends like Tandra helping me out, it helps."

Ria could have knocked Tandra out right there in the street. But she decided to stay a lady. Ria did not expect that type of betrayal from her. She knew that she had been acting cold toward her, but this was low of her.

"Well, I must dash. I have a few more things to pick up. I will probably see you both this Saturday." Andréa looked inquisitively at Ria. "Oh, didn't Tandra or Shawn tell you? I'm having a party for Jackson's first birthday."

Andréa shot Tandra a look that could freeze water. Before Tandra could speak, Ria interrupted, "Like I said, I have to go. See you then." Ria continued walking, she was surprised on how she felt. She harbored a little jealousy for Andrea but no hate. It was obvious now that Shawn had moved on with his life and so had she. Her day still felt beautiful, and the sun still felt like it was on her side.

Chapter Thirty-Six

James knocked on Ria's office door before entering. "Can I come in please, for a little talk?"

Ria looked up, mid sip of her latte, and placed the cup back on her desk

"Oh James," she said, "get your butt in here."

James entered with a smile and closed Ria's office door. Ria observed his posture and braced herself. It wasn't like James to have such a formal approach for a little talk.

"I just wanted to see if you were all right."

"All right about what?"

"Well, it's all over the office that Shawn is getting married."

"That's old news. Of course I'm okay. There may be a lot of history between Shawn and me, but that's what it is—history!" James gazed at Ria. "You are an astonishing woman."

"Thank you very much," Ria said, imitating Elvis.

"Promise me one thing. If we're both single when you're forty, you will marry me."

"Oh, of course, I promise." James winked at Ria, then returned back to his office, leaving Ria's door ajar.

The talk of Shawn's wedding made Ria wonder what he saw in Andréa. She could see that she was almost the opposite of herself. Ria walked across her office and closed the door. She had yet to tell Cissy about yesterday's meeting with Tandra and Andréa. Ria dialed Cissy's cell phone number, Cissy picked up the call on the first ring.

"Hey, can you talk?" Ria said.

"Yeah, what's up, Ri?" Cissy said.

"Guess who's thrown a dagger in my back?"

"Who?" Cissy said.

"Tandra. I saw her with Shawn's fiancé, walking together, picking out bridal dresses." Ria said.

"Are you kidding me? I had a feeling she had a trifling edge to her." Even though Ria tried to stay optimistic, the residue of what happened yesterday left her ego dented. Her man was gone and now her girlfriend. All by the same woman.

*****

It was Saturday morning, and Andréa lay in bed on her side. Her hazel eyes stayed fixated on Shawn who was miles away in sleep land. It felt good to wake up alongside the man of her dreams. She often wondered whether he was worth the sacrifice. As she continued to stare at Shawn, the phone rang, which made Shawn stir out of his sleep. The phone was on his side of the bed, so he sleepily stretched over and picked it up.

"Hello?" Shawn said in a deep baritone voice. He glanced at Andréa, wondering why she was staring at him.

"Shawn," the voice said over the phone, "it's Kenny."

"Where are you? You've got a lot to answer to. What were you thinking? You could have harmed Andréa."

"I know, that's why I turned myself in," Kenny said regretfully.

Andréa lay beside Shawn with her arm on his bare chest. She did not bother to ask him about his son's birthday party. The party was later on that day, and she was quite confident that he would tell her when he had the chance. Tandra had given Andréa a sorry excuse of forgetting and that she had no intention of going. Andréa started to question Tandra's authenticity as a friend. Even though Andréa had distanced herself from most of her friends, she wondered whether she needed to do the same with her. But then again, maybe it would be best to keep her as an insider.

"I hate to see you locked up," Shawn said, sighing. "What type

of life is that?"

"Look, Shawn, right now, it's the best place for me to be. They're going to put me on an intensive drug program.

"I can find a similar program," Shawn said.

"No, bro, I have to do it this way."

"I'm getting married in six weeks. I want you to be there as my best man." Shawn said.

"That's nice, Shawn, but what type of best man have I been to you?"

"That's not the point…"

"Shawn, I've got to go. My time is up. I'll see you when I see you…"

"But what penitentiary are you in?" The line went dead.

Shawn held his hand to his head. Andréa gently guided him toward her chest and gave him a hug. "Don't worry, baby. He'll be all right."

After a couple of minutes, Shawn released himself from Andréa's embrace. "I've got to get some fresh air."

"Where are you going, honey? I wanted to discuss the last preparations for the wedding with you," Andréa said as her eyes followed Shawn from the bed.

"I just received a call from my brother who is incarcerated, and you want me to talk about a wedding? Are you crazy?"

"Baby, I'm sorry. That was insensitive of me. Stay, I'll give you a nice back massage."

"No, I'm going to see my son," Shawn said with irritation.

He stripped off his boxers and stepped into the walk-in shower. The water didn't help in washing away his frustration. Shawn knew he had everything—a nice car, home, money, but he was not happy. It seemed that since breaking up with Ria, everything apart from his career had turned into a mess. He needed her so badly in times like this. After almost two years, Shawn's heart still ached for her.

Shawn came out of the shower and took out a white T-shirt and a pair of jeans. He looked at Andrea's forlorn expression. He hadn't meant to hurt her.

"Look, it's Jackson's first birthday today, and I want to go and spend some time with him. When I get back, I promise we'll talk about the wedding, okay?"

"Okay," Andréa said as though she was a child.

It was this type of sharing that got on Andrea's nerves, every moment Shawn had to spend with Ria made her nervous. But soon she would be married to him, a perfect family, she would have his child and what contest would there be then.

Chapter Thirty-Seven

ackson's party was in full swing. Kids from his play group were running up and down the garden while Desiree and her friends jumped up and down on a bouncy castle that was positioned at the corner of the garden. The two white canopies on both sides of Chanel's garden sheltered tables of food and salads. Steve, Chanel's husband, was over at the barbecue, flipping burgers and pork ribs like a pro. Quite a few church members arrived with their children, and Ria wondered if she had prepared enough food.

Everybody seemed to be enjoying themselves, apart from Jackson. He was irritable and would not settle. Every time Ria attempted to put him down to enjoy an activity, he would start to cry. Clara looked on helplessly.

"Oh, Jackson, what's the matter? It's your birthday, you should be happy," she said while Jackson clung to his mother even more.

"I don't know what his problem is," Ria said, annoyed.

Suddenly, Jackson's face lit up, and he started stretching out his arms toward Ria's shoulder. Ria turned around to find out what had changed his tune. It was Shawn carrying a huge object in his arms. He placed it down by the entrance of the garden. Ria placed Jackson down, and he attempted to walk toward his father. "I'll be back in a minute. I'm just going to greet Jackson's father," Ria said to Clara whose mouth dropped open. She had yet to inform Clara that Jackson's father was a professional footballer. By the look on Clara's face, Ria was glad she hadn't mentioned it earlier.

Ria walked behind Jackson to catch him before he fell. He was trying to run before he had mastered the art of walking. She smiled at Shawn, trying to act as normal as possible. She could not help but make that extra effort in her appearance; she knew he was coming.

"Hey, you're early. I was not expecting you to come until much later."

"Why would I miss out on spending the day with Jackson on his first birthday?" As he bent down to kiss her on her cheek, he was amazed at how good Ria looked. Her burnt orange halter neck top complemented her skin tone. The orange rose she wore on the side of her curly hair brought back that youthfulness he was used to seeing on her.

"Well, I thought you'd be busy, planning a wedding and all…" Ria said with a slight sarcastic tone. Shawn frowned.

"What? Was it something I said?"

Shawn picked up Jackson and elevated him above his head, then lowered him back down. Jackson giggled.

"Who told you that I was getting married?" Shawn said aggravated. He did not want the news getting out all over Los Angeles.

"I bumped into Tandra and your fiancé earlier this week."

"What's Tandra doing with Andréa?" Shawn asked baffled by the association.

"I have no idea," Ria said. She did not want to go into Tandra's backstabbing drama on her son's birthday.

"I'm sorry I did not have the chance to tell you," Shawn said softly as he lowered his tone.

"You don't need to apologize. It's none of my business." She touched his arm.

A bad odor wafted past Ria's nose, and she knew that odor could only belong to Jackson. "Boy, have you done a doo-doo." She moved her nose closer to Jackson's bottom as Shawn held him. Jackson shook his head innocently at his mother. "Yes, you did, you smelly boy. Come let me change you before you run all these people out of this yard."

Jackson began to cry and held on to his dad. "It's okay, I'll come up with you," Shawn said. As Ria led the way upstairs to the guest room, Shawn followed while holding Jackson. She laid the changing mat on the bed while Shawn lay his son down on it.

"I'm not sure if I can go through with the wedding," Shawn muttered.

Ria lifted her eyebrow at Shawn's sudden announcement. She continued to drag baby wipes from the packet and clean up Jackson's messy bottom. She did not want to know why or what was going on in Shawn's love life.

"Am I the right person to be discussing this with? It's really none of my business," Ria said. After the Tandra and Andréa situation, she really did not want to get more involved than she already was in Shawn's drama.

"You don't understand…"

"Understand what?" Ria said with a slight snap in her tone.

Ria pulled Jackson's pants up and handed him back to Shawn. She quickly packed up the baby wipes and shoved the changing mat in the small closet by the bed.

"I don't love Andréa. I've been in love with another woman all along."

Ria stopped and turned back around to face Shawn. Shawn still sat on the bed holding Jackson. Ria really struggled now; she was not going to stay and listen to Shawn pour out his heart about another women. It had taken her awhile to get used to Andréa. She didn't even want to deal with another woman.

"Shawn, are you sure you should be discussing this with me?" Ria asked again. Jackson lifted Shawn's cell phone and pointed at the face of it and waited for his father's response. Shawn responded with a smile. "Yes, son, you want to call one of your friends?"

The little interruption from Jackson gave Ria the perfect chance to escape. "I better get back downstairs and see how things are going."

"Ria, please. I need to tell you something." Ria sat on the bed. "What is it, Shawn?"

"The woman I've always loved is you. I can't get you out of my mind. And I need you back. The other night…"

Ria softly held her hand to her neck in an attempt to stop her from choking. She could feel the blood circulating around her body at a fast rate.

She glanced at Shawn, at a loss for words. She refused to look into his eyes. She didn't want to lose herself in them. She turned her attention to her son and then the floor in order to break the intensity of the pressure she was feeling in her body.

"How dare you come at me with that," she said. "You have placed a ring on another woman's finger that is walking around looking for a wedding dress and you are telling me now that you love me."

"The other night made me see how beautiful it would be if we were back together as a family. It takes one look at Jackson or seeing you and bang I'm back there."

Ria did not want to hear this. She had just got her life together as a single woman. Her emotions and heart had just started to stabilized.

"Too much has changed between us, Shawn. We have a beautiful son to prove it. Let's just leave it to that." Ria shook her head as though she was trying to convince herself. "No, I can't go through that emotional rollercoaster again."

"I can't help but kick myself for letting you go. It was my fault why we broke up not yours. If I wasn't acting like a jerk I would have realized that you are the only woman for me. Everything we had dreamed about doing is right here. We're a family now isn't that what we wanted?"

Ria was doing well until that statement. She could not deny it; Ria still loved Shawn, and the words that she was hearing felt like soothing balm to her soul.

"Look, we can get away from all of this craziness," Shawn said. "We'll move to the country, get married, and get back to the way things used to be. I have enough money for us to live comfortably."

"You think it's going to be that easy, Shawn? And what are we

going to do in the country, huh?"

"Well okay not the country, anywhere you want to be, and where we can be a family."

Ria shook her head. "I-I'm not the same woman that you let go two years ago," Ria said, her eyes welling with tears. "I had built my life so much around you that I didn't know who I was. I've moved on physically, emotionally, and spiritually. I'm sorry, but it can't happen." Ria managed to restrict her tears from falling down her cheeks.

"I love you," Shawn said, trying desperately to look into Ria's eyes. She avoided his like the plague.

"Shawn, I think you better leave."

Ria got up from her seat and took Jackson from Shawn. She snatched his cell phone from her son and threw it on the bed. Jackson started to cry. "You will always have a spot in my heart, but you and I cannot work."

Shawn reached for Ria's hand to stop her from walking out. Ria stopped and turned. She was so close to Shawn that she could feel his breath on her face. She could no longer hide her emotions now, being so close to him. His aftershave and

warmth cocooned her. She was captured by the sincerity of his eyes. This time she tasted the saltiness of her tears. Jackson calmed at the nearness of both his father and mother.

Shawn touched Ria's lower back, she closed her eyes slowly. It felt good to be held by Shawn again. Shawn knew Ria was caving into his advances. He decided to move even closer to Ria until his nose touched hers. It felt so natural and easy to hold the woman he loved. He did not have to try hard to love Ria.

"I'll break it off with Andréa tonight and then we can work on us being a family," he said. "I'm in love with you and even more so with the woman you have become."

Ria felt the softness of Shawn's lips, she completely forgot about all the drama that surrounded him. Ria allowed her hormones to get the best of her and her guard was totally down.

"We better get back down stairs," she whispered. "We've been up here awhile."

"I'm going to go and sort things at home. I'll call you tonight?" Shawn rubbed Ria's lower back. "Y—yeah. Can you take Jackson downstairs? I just need to freshen up my face." Shawn nodded, collected Jackson in his arms, and left the room.

The noise from the garden echoed into the room. Ria took a sneak peak out of the window which gave a good view of the garden without being noticed. She realized from her view that the garden which was formally half full was peppered with more people. Ria watched as Shawn departed out of the garden and out of the house before she got the courage to return to her son's party.

Chapter Thirty-Eight

The scent of three huge ginger and orange candles danced from three corners of the low lit bathroom. Hot steam protruded out of the shower like a boiling cauldron; the movements of two individuals were shadowed on the walls.

"You seemed to be in a happy mood," Traci said as she embraced Daniel from behind in the glass walled shower. It was a long time since they had a romantic evening.

"Things are looking up for me now."

"Well for both of us," Traci said as she rubbed the soap lather into Daniel's back. "I was thinking, why we don't get away for a couple of days, just the two of us."

"Huh?" Daniel said as he turned to face Traci.

"You know maybe the Grand Canyon or San Diego."

"That would be nice for Christmas."

"Christmas? That's months away. I'm talking about next weekend, silly."

"You should have said something before, baby. I would have booked it up for us to go. We can go away for Christmas. What you think of Hawaii?" Daniel embraced her and smoothed the soap lather onto her body as they passionately kissed and made love.

Tyler had contacted Daniel and invited him down to Las Vegas for a 'meeting.' Daniel could not do it; he knew where it would lead him. He remembered the saying curiosity killed the cat and he was not willing to fall the victim to that again. Having a stable home, a wife that he was falling in love with again was all he needed.

It was seven o'clock in the evening and the summer sun simmered down on the horizon as if it was melting into the sky. Andréa walked slowly unto each step that led to her church door. It had been almost a year since she last attended a full service. It felt strange. She took a deep breath as she went around the back side door which led straight to Pastor Michael's office. She really did not want to bump into anyone familiar and have to lie as to why she had been away for so long. Just the entrance of the church made her feel repentant. Even though she had not booked an appointment to see her pastor, she thought she would chance it knowing that Saturdays were counseling days.

Andréa glanced around the slim corridor, she had a sense of longing. She almost passed the side door of the main hall, but decided to stop and take a peek inside the empty hall. She opened the door and was compelled to take a seat. She made her way to her favorite seat. Seat number twenty-four. The one that the ushers saved for her every Wednesday and Sunday. Now that her absence had been present for over a year, she wondered who had taken her seat. As her bottom pressed down unto the cushioned burgundy seat, she felt a slight awkwardness. She leaned forward and placed her handbag on the adjacent chair. Softly playing in the background was Marvin Sapp's *Thirsty*. It set the mood for Andréa and she felt more welcomed than rebuked.

The atmosphere was sweet and she felt light in her soul. She allowed the words of the song to soothe her. It seemed every word was what she wanted to say to God. Andréa desperately wanted a blessing for her wedding, but the sleepless nights and her conscience was beginning to take its toll on whether she was doing the right thing. Andréa could not believe the woman she had become. Never in the million years did she think she would be involved in any baby mama drama.

Even her friendship with Tandra plagued her conscience. She wanted to be that sweet spirited woman she once was. Being with Shawn had cost her, her closet friends, and most of all her relationship with God. Now alone in the house of God, no Shawn

and no Ria taking up her thoughts, she had clarity. Andréa remembered her passion to teach young women how to cook. She also wanted to open up a soup kitchen to feed the homeless. All of her dreams and aspirations seemed to have been taken over by Shawn. She wondered how she got so wrapped up in him. It was easy to reflect and examine the woman she had become in such an atmosphere.

While the music continued to play, it ministered to her in an area of her soul that she had neglected. The part that did not recover from her devastation and pain. Andréa missed that place of confidence she had in her faith. She had two choices now before her, one that would have her play someone's second best and the other even though single, be loved by the One who could love and heal her.

Andréa opened her hazel eyes and looked at the red carpet which lay in front of the pulpit. It reminded her of the color of blood, the blood that was shed for her sins. It made her think about when she first gave her life to Christ, a second chance was given to her. Andréa knew in her spirit that another one was being presented to her. Letting go of Shawn would lead her to pain that could take her a season to get over. But waiting for him to hurt her was a torture she just could not bear to live with. Andréa got up from her twenty-fourth seat; she had no need to see Pastor Michael. She knew the answer and had received the blessing she needed to continue her journey.

*****

It was ten o'clock in the evening and Jackson's party had dwindled down to Cissy, Clara, Chanel, and Ria. Chanel's husband had retired for the evening and both Desiree and Jackson lay in the living room. The quartet were still outside enjoying the warm summer heat, dancing to the rare groove music playing on the outside speakers.

"Oh girls! It's been too long since I have been able to shake my butt like this. It feels good to cut some rug," Ria said, getting

lost in her dance to *Forget Me Nots*.

"Don't you mean cut the grass, girl?" Chanel asked as she mirrored her sister's moves.

"Whatever! Come on, Cissy, you can't be sitting out on us. Doesn't this song remind you of your heyday?"

Ria reached for Cissy's hand and pulled her up on her bare feet. Cissy reluctantly got up from her recliner garden chair and slowly got into the groove.

"Now this is my jam! *What ya thinka, what ya feel now... too real be real.* That Cheryl Lynn can sing. We gotta do soul train to this, girls," Cissy said as she lined up with the rest of the girls.

"Clara, you can do soul train?" Chanel said in disbelief.

"You can take the girl out the club, but you can't take the groove out of the girl," Clara said while laughing.

"You know that don't make no sense at all," Ria said, amused by Clara's catchphrase.

"So, Mami, what were you and Shawn talking about earlier on for so long?"

"None of your business, Chanel," Ria said, laughing.

"It is my business when you're in my house. I hope y'all never did any quickies in my spare room."

Clara looked at Chanel in amazement. She was not used to hearing Chanel speak with such attitude. "Can we concentrate on the dance please?" Ria asked. "You're messing it up. To the left to the right, now back."

Ria's cell phone vibrated in her back pocket, and she broke the synchronized boogie to answer it. "Hello Ria speaking?"

"Ria! Look it's Jonathan. Shawn's been in an accident, a real bad accident and has been rushed to the intensive care unit."

"Accident! How... when... he was at my place just this afternoon. I thought he was going straight home." Chanel, Cissy, and Clara looked on with concern.

"I will tell you the rest when you get to the hospital."

"I'm on my way." Ria placed her cell back in her back pocket. She spun around in the grass, looking absentmindedly for her shoes.

"What, what's the matter, Ri?" Chanel asked.

"It's Shawn. He's been in an accident and has been rushed to the hospital. I don't know how it happened. All I know is that I've got to get to the hospital."

"Oh my goodness," Chanel said. "I'll come with you. You can't drive in your state. Cissy, can you stay and watch over the kids?"

"Of course," Cissy said.

Chanel watched Ria as the tears pilled in her eyes. She hugged her sister and whispered, "It will be OK." Ria stared at her, half-believing.

"It will be," Chanel repeated.

In the car, Chanel kept staring over at Ria, who hugged herself tightly and rocked.

"I'm sure it's not as serious as it sounds, Ria," she said. "Don't worry. He'll be all right."

"How can you say that, Chanel? You don't even know. Jonathan sounded so shaken up." On the freeway, they slowly past an accident scene scattered with petrol vehicles and police cars.

"Oh my God," Ria yelled. "There's Shawn's car. Please God, don't let him die, don't let him die."

"Let's just get to the hospital, honey, okay?" Chanel asked.

Ria didn't respond. She could only continue rocking and praying for Shawn's life.

*****

It was not too long before they reached the hospital. Before Chanel had a chance to park the car, Ria jumped out and sprinted inside. She reached the reception with a surge of adrenalin that pumped through her body, making her feel light headed.

"Excuse me," she said to the woman behind the desk. She struggled to catch her breath. "Could you please tell me where Shawn Matthews is? He was brought here from an accident."

The lady looked on her computer and directed Ria to the correct floor. It was not that long ago that she was at the same

hospital with Shawn to see Kenny; it all seemed like déjà vu. Ria wished in her heart that it was Kenny and not Shawn laid up in hospital. As she approached the room, she saw Jonathan with a distraught look on his face. She ran to hug him.

"Where is he? I want to see him." Ria went to run into the theatre room, but Jonathan pulled her back and held her in his arms. "What's happening, Jonathan? Tell me what's happening."

"I don't know. He's in surgery now. The doctor said something about his heart. We have to wait for the doctor. He'll be out soon."

Chanel entered the room and held Ria who was still hanging on to Jonathan. She was shaking like a frightened little child. Chanel managed to guide her to the seating area while Jonathan remained standing; he then returned to pacing from one length of the room to another.

"What and how did the accident happened?" Chanel asked Jonathan.

"I was driving just behind him." Jonathan shook his head, wrung his hands. "We were going to go to the bar and all of a sudden a car shot right in front of him and as he tried to swerve, he just h-he just ran into the side." Jonathan spoke his words to the air around him, his attention not on Chanel, on anything.

"What happened to the other driver?"

"He drove just drove, he just drove off. I-I did not know what to do. I was in shock."

"Did you get a view of what he looked like?" Chanel asked, still rocking Ria side to side as though she was calming a baby.

"He kinda look liked... man, I don't know."

"He looked like who?" Ria asked sternly. Jonathan drew his attention from the ceiling and gazed at Ria.

"He looked like...like Kenny, I mean I don't know. It was dark and it all happened so quickly."

Jonathan noticed the look of hatred that swept over Ria's expression before she buried her face back into her sister's bosom.

Andréa rushed through the hospital doors where she was directed. She could not quite understand the voice message that

Jonathan had left on her cell phone. But she knew it was something about a car accident. As she came near the doors, she heard a blood curdling wail. The sound cut her like a knife, and tears began to fall down her face. It could not be Shawn, she thought. But as she entered the room, she saw Ria deranged and on the floor screaming. Andréa was not sure whether it was Jackson or Shawn that had been hurt.

She walked up to Jonathan, who had his hands on his head. He shook his head and said, "I'm sorry, Andrea. Shawn is g-gone. He's dead."

Unable to comprehend what she had heard, Andrea walked out of the room and stood just outside of it. She could not breathe and was gasping for air.

Her mouth started to water. Before she could control it, she was vomiting on the hospital floor just outside of the meeting room. One of the nurses ran to her aid with tissue. As the nurse guided her to a seat, Andréa sat down down calmly but was unable to respond to the nurse's questions. She was unable to cry, scream or talk.

"It can't be Shawn," she muttered. "No, he can't be dead."

Andréa used the tissue to wipe the vomit from her mouth and chin. She could not comprehend what had happened.

"Excuse me, ma'am, are you okay?" the nurse asked while still sitting beside Andréa.

"I've got to see him."

Andréa stood, leaving the comforting nurse in limbo and walked back into the room. There she saw Ria sitting with her sister, eyes swollen as she looked to the ground. Ria still had not noticed her.

"I should have told him I loved him when I had the chance," Ria said. "He wanted to make a new start, he wanted to be a family." Ria wiped the tears from her face. "That's what we spoke about today. I should have told him... I-I loved him."

Chanel had seen Andréa and tried to prevent Ria from saying more by placing Ria's head on her bosom and rocking her slowly.

"Shhhh, Ria," she said. "Don't blame yourself."

Unable to find an emotion before, Andréa's eyes filled with pain and agony. Jonathan walked up to Andréa, and with the dignity she had left, she prevented herself from breaking down.

"Please can I see him?" Andréa asked Jonathan quietly.

Andréa felt Ria's eyes leave the floor and penetrate into her back as she walked past her. Andréa was not willing to have any confrontation. What was the point? Ria had won. Knowing Ria was the apple of Shawn's eye was not surprising to her, but it still hurt like hell. Jonathan took her hand and led her into the room. She walked slowly to the bed and wished Shawn was alive so she could smack him in the mouth. Instead, she touched his lifeless face and bent down to kiss him on the forehead. She had no choice now but to continue the path she chose while sitting in church.

As she walked out calmly, Ria glanced at Andréa and as their eyes met, they locked. Andréa held her gaze on Ria while she wiped an escaped tear which swam down her cheek. Andréa walked over to Ria. The sorrow that she saw in Ria's eyes was almost as overwhelming as seeing Shawn's lifeless body on the bed. The very woman she was trying to compete with had transformed into a grieving widow, with a child who was now fatherless. Even though Andréa was filled with pain, she still had a peace that strengthened her. Andréa knew she had to say something, something that would help her close a painful season of being second best.

Tapping back into her old self, she knew that only the truth would set her free. She bent down and whispered to Ria, "You were the only woman Shawn ever loved. I hope you know that." Andrea said. She touched Ria's quivering hand affectionately and then continued to walk through the doors without looking back.

Dear Reader,

Thank you for reading my novel. I hope you enjoyed it. I always appreciate the time people take in reading my projects. I love getting feedback from readers, so connect with me on Facebook or email me at EvaGHeadley@hotmail.co.uk. The sequel to Tied to the Soul is in the works so visit my website to stay updated.

Eva
EvaGHeadley.com

Eva G Headley

Author, Writer and Poet

Eva G Headley resides in the UK. She is a passionate author and poet who loves writing inspirational novels and short stories that have unexpected endings and juicy storylines. Her next novel, Twisted Fantasy, will release in 2012.

Eva is the founder of Got 2 Get Hitched Ministries and presents on the topic of singlehood. Eva is not afraid to speak out about the realities of singleness or approach controversial issues of being single in the city.

Visit her website EvaGHeadley.com to purchase short stories and email her on EvaGHeadley@hotmail.co.uk. You can also connect with her on Facebook.com/Eva.G.Headley.

The Write to Inspire Publishing Company (WIP) publishes inspirational, creative, and touching stories which leave its reader reflecting on their own lives while still maintaining an entertaining page turner.

We are looking to publish Romance, Inspirational, Urban and Young adult fiction in the capacity of short stories (e-books) and novels. For more information please visit our website www.thewritetoinspire.com.

Recommended Reads

Author Norma L. Jarrett

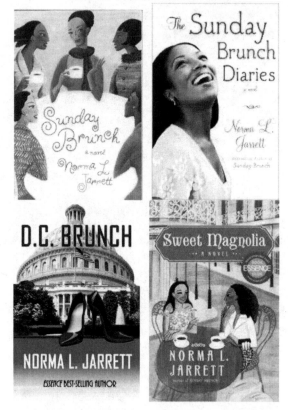

Lexi, Capri, Jermane, Angel, and Jewel are back together meeting on Sundays to chat about their lives, the law and the Lord. Each woman has tried to keep the faith and follow her dream—and each has discovered that sometimes when your prayers are answered you get much more than you bargained for. Will Lexi and Capri's friendship survive a new business partnership? Can Jermane and husband, Rex, keep their marriage fresh despite his workaholic ways and wandering eyes? And will differences in faith drive Angel and her new boyfriend apart? For information about Essence bestselling author, Norma L Jarrett, visit NormaJarrett.net.